REST IN THE RAINBOW

Finding Strength and Purpose in the Promises of God

STEPHANIE SCHLUETER

WESTBOW
PRESS®
A DIVISION OF THOMAS NELSON
& ZONDERVAN

Copyright © 2022 Stephanie Schlueter.

All rights reserved. No part of this book may be used or reproduced by any means, graphic, electronic, or mechanical, including photocopying, recording, taping or by any information storage retrieval system without the written permission of the author except in the case of brief quotations embodied in critical articles and reviews.

WestBow Press books may be ordered through booksellers or by contacting:

WestBow Press
A Division of Thomas Nelson & Zondervan
1663 Liberty Drive
Bloomington, IN 47403
www.westbowpress.com
844-714-3454

Because of the dynamic nature of the Internet, any web addresses or links contained in this book may have changed since publication and may no longer be valid. The views expressed in this work are solely those of the author and do not necessarily reflect the views of the publisher, and the publisher hereby disclaims any responsibility for them.

Any people depicted in stock imagery provided by Getty Images are models, and such images are being used for illustrative purposes only. Certain stock imagery © Getty Images.

The Christian Standard Bible. Copyright © 2017 by Holman Bible Publishers. Used by permission. Christian Standard Bible®, and CSB® are federally registered trademarks of Holman Bible Publishers, all rights reserved.

Scripture quotations taken from The Holy Bible, New International Version® NIV® Copyright © 1973 1978 1984 2011 by Biblica, Inc. TM. Used by permission. All rights reserved worldwide.

ISBN: 978-1-6642-5613-2 (sc)
ISBN: 978-1-6642-5614-9 (hc)
ISBN: 978-1-6642-5612-5 (e)

Library of Congress Control Number: 2022901526

Print information available on the last page.

WestBow Press rev. date: 02/04/2022

In memory of Kaye Scaggs.
Thank you for showing us how to use our God-given gifts and be extensions of God's love and grace in this world.

CONTENTS

Prologue ix
Introduction: Proof of a Promise xiii

PART 1: ALIGNMENT 1
Chapter 1   Unlearning 3
Chapter 2   Back to the Basics 11
Chapter 3   Identity Crisis 19
Chapter 4   Studying for a Test You've Already Passed 35
Chapter 5   Pain in Perspective 45
Chapter 6   Step into the Ring 54
Chapter 7   Functional Faith 62
Chapter 8   Drop Your Anchor 70
Chapter 9   Remember Your Stones 78

PART 2: ASSIGNMENT 85
Chapter 10   Love Language 89
Chapter 11   A Kingdom Mindset 99
Chapter 12   Living in the Tension 110
Chapter 13   Be the Light and Throw Salt 124
Chapter 14   Unwrapping Your Gift 141
Chapter 15   Heavenly Assignment 150

Bibliography 165

PROLOGUE

Hardship looks different for everyone, and we are all fighting battles others know nothing about. Some of our deepest valleys may look like sickness, loss of a loved one, divorce, depression, financial distress, or a combination of more than one. My deepest valley consisted of fifteen years of chronic illness. I will reference my battle with my health several times throughout this book; this is because my journey with ulcerative colitis, an autoimmune disease, has been my biggest testimony as a witness to God's grace and power. My faith was built in a valley of sickness and despair. The most valuable lesson I learned through the deepest valley of my life is that God has to work in you, so He can work through you. The last few years of my life have been full of learning more about God, building my trust in Him, dwelling on His promises, as well as the physical and spiritual healing I desperately needed. I realized that the time of sickness and the period of waiting actually turned out to be a time of discipline and alignment of God's will for my life.

The work God did in me, aligning me with His will and perspective, has allowed me to step into my true voice and invest in the spiritual gifts He has given me, so I can walk in the calling the Lord has put in my heart. Adversity actually deepened my insight and helped me better understand my identity. My identity is in Him. It's not who I am, but Whose I am. It's no longer about me. It's about Him. It's about you.

My goal for this book is to help you understand that there is so much power in God's promises. But in order to experience their power, you have to claim them. You must dwell on them. You have to let God's voice be the loudest one in your life. Claiming God's promises is the first step to unlocking the gift of peace and joy that will carry you through the stormiest seasons in your life. My other goal for this book is to show you how to claim God's promises and walk in who He has called you to be.

Our true heavenly purpose begins to unfold once we decide to pursue Jesus boldly. It's learning that while faith is about hope, it's also about believing that God's promises are your guide and anchor in navigating this world. It's about allowing Him to use His truths to cultivate your heart to be more like His. It's about listening to that soft whisper that prompts you to answer your calling.

Jesus said that many are invited, but few are chosen. Not because God shows favoritism, but the difference between the called and the chosen is that the chosen ones are those who choose to answer their calling (Evans, 305).

You have a calling. But it begins with a choice. There's no secret formula. Jesus wants your heart so He can pour His Spirit and revelations into you and teach you how He wants you to shine your light and accomplish your heavenly assignment in this world.

This book is the result of an answer to my calling.

This book is for you. I am only writing this book as God's messenger. I have prayed over this book and spent countless hours writing, seeking the Lord's guidance and making sure every word poured out on these pages is a direct reflection of God and His convicting heart.

I hope and pray that this book teaches you how to find strength and purpose in God's promises and encourages you to pursue Jesus with more boldness than you ever have. I challenge you to open your heart and see yourself the way God sees you. I challenge you to love yourself, and love others, the way God desires us to. God wants to use you in ways beyond imagination. You will be surprised at what God will show you, if you allow Him into your heart and spend time with Him.

He is after your heart.

I hope the words of this book chase you down and wrap you up in His mighty love and conviction.

INTRODUCTION: PROOF OF A PROMISE

> I have placed my bow in the clouds, and it will be a sign of the covenant between me and the earth. Whenever I form clouds over the earth and the bow appears in the clouds, I will remember my covenant between me and you and all the living creatures: water will never again become a flood to destroy every creature. (Genesis 9:13–15)

A covenant is a promise, and God was talking about a rainbow. This was one of the first promises God made to us in the Bible. Before this promise was recorded, God had wiped out the entire earth and all living creatures by water—with the exception of the passengers (both people and animals) on the ark God instructed Noah to build before the Flood. Once the Flood was over, which took about a year, Noah and his passengers arrived safely on dry land.

God promised to never take the earth by flood again, and He meant it. Just as He means all of the thousands of promises recorded in scripture.

It's pretty cool that God left us a visible reminder of His promises.

Rainbows serve as a reminder that God is still present, and He is still using the beauty of nature to illustrate His promises to us. Some may look at rainbows as a natural phenomenon, but God put a rainbow in the sky long before it was claimed by science.

Rainbows got me through the most difficult season of my life, and they are also the reason for the title of this book. In 2019, I went through a series of three reconstructive bowel surgeries, after a fifteen-year battle with ulcerative colitis. The two years prior to my surgeries were long and hard-fought, and I eventually got to a point where I was physically losing the war against my own body. My body had stopped responding to any and all medicine used to treat ulcerative colitis.

During these two painful years prior to my surgeries, I cried a lot. I prayed a lot. I asked God to show me purpose and give me understanding as to why I had to suffer so much. I was so confused. I believed God was good, and I knew it, but it was a terrifying, sinking feeling to see my body physically wearing out. My symptoms were becoming unmanageable, and the amount of immune-suppressant medication I was taking only made me more susceptible to other sickness and infection. What made the feeling more dooming was that I was told over and over again by medical experts that surgery was impossible for me. I knew I was running out of treatment options.

I was tired, but I made a deliberate effort not to consume myself with negative thoughts. I made a promise to God that no matter how hard it was, I was going to put my confidence and trust in Him. I prayed for strength. Every time I started to get upset, and every time the familiar thoughts of fear and worry crept up in my mind, I would hear that small, quiet voice say, "Keep pushing. Don't give up."

I know that was God. And I promise you, that voice was the only thing that kept me going.

Fast-forward to 2019—I sought a second opinion from another gastroenterologist, who told me that reconstructive surgery was my last (and only) option. He scheduled my first surgery three weeks later. This doctor was also my surgeon. The day I scheduled my first surgery was not only the day God answered my prayers, but it was also the day that the connection between my pain and His promises became so clear. Although I wasn't out of the valley, I will never forget the moment that peace washed over me the day I left my new doctor's office.

A lot of times, we find ourselves asking God, why? Why must we go through seasons that bring us to our breaking points?

The answer to that question is this:

God allows adversity in our lives in order to teach us how to trust Him. He allows adversity to test our faith, because He wants us to be fully dependent on Him. He knows that full dependence on Him requires us to surrender control of our circumstances. God isn't offended or surprised by your questions, but if you ever catch yourself asking "why," then He may be trying to get your attention. One thing I've learned in my battle with my health over the last fifteen years is that God doesn't respond to pain; He responds to faithfulness. The Lord is committed to meeting our needs, but He wants to know first if we trust Him to do so. The beautiful part about adversity, though, is that He never calls us to go it alone, and He will never let the enemy destroy us. God puts limitations on adversity so that when we lean on Him, the end result is spiritual strength and confidence. By reading this paragraph alone, you have just read five more promises from the Word of God.

Faith shouldn't be our last resort; it should be our first instinct.

The Bible is full of stories of people who went through some incredibly tough times. They describe what happens when people listen to God's instruction, follow Him, and look to Him for direction and wisdom. These stories are filled with breakthroughs, miracles, and redemption. They are testimonies of not only God's supernatural power, but of the strength of what a promise from God actually means.

Do you know what these ordinary people relied on during their trials and suffering?

God's promises.

Do you know what Jesus said to Satan when He was tempted for forty days in the desert after He was baptized?

"It is written."

Even Jesus used the Word of God as His battle weapon. God does not break His promises. It is a firm foundation of truth and faithfulness.

Before I go any further, I want to explain to you why we can absolutely trust and believe in what the Bible says. Some people are skeptical about its reliability, and I've got a few words for you: Cross-references and prophetic fulfillment.

There are over three hundred thousand cross-references in the Bible. A cross-reference is a piece of scripture that refers to another piece of scripture, between the Old Testament (before Jesus came to earth) and the New Testament (during and after Jesus's time on earth). What makes this so interesting and amazing is that the Bible has forty different authors and was written over the span of fifteen hundred years. In addition to these cross-references, every promise in the Bible that has been prophesied has been fulfilled, without a margin of error. Prophetic fulfillment has had a perfect track record throughout history. Prophets in the Bible have accurately predicted events in great detail, years and centuries before they occurred. In fact, approximately two thousand of the twenty-five hundred prophecies in the pages of the Bible have already been fulfilled.

What's even more fascinating about these numbers is that, as I mentioned, the Bible has forty different authors, who all grew up in different time periods throughout this fifteen-hundred-year time span. If you break down the statistics, the probability of all those prophecies being fulfilled, without error, is so small that I don't even know the proper terminology to explain how small of a number that is; it's pretty much impossible. Humankind cannot produce that level of statistical significance. But I believe God works in ways that make you understand that He is in control, and nothing is impossible for the One Who created the world.

The Bible is the most reliable history book we have. I can give you three hundred thousand reasons why.

I remember when I first picked up a Bible. It was in 2012, and I was in another very dark season of my life. I remember saying, "God,

I really don't know how to pray. Don't you already know what I'm thinking anyways? You should already know what I need. I don't really understand what I'm reading, but here we are, so I'm gonna give this a shot."

Gradually, things started to make a little sense. I started to connect the dots. I wasn't always faithful in spending time with God, but I kept working at it. As time went on, I would stray from God for a while and then come back to Him. But then, the time gaps between myself and time spent with God began to get shorter and shorter. I began to realize how much I was starting to rely on God's promises in the Bible. I started to realize how much I needed those affirmations of unconditional love and comfort, and I realized how much I needed those promises to give me strength and endurance through my seasons of tough times.

As I pressed more into Him, He showed me even more about who He is. I was able to have better discernment of that still, soft voice. He spoke to me in ways that can't be explained, only felt. I started falling in love with God. As I fell more in love with Him, I fell more in love with myself. I was able to love myself more because I invested in the truth, that God gave me boundless grace to pay my way into heaven, and it was also enough grace for me to forgive myself for being a victim to a broken, corrupt world. It was a type of grace that convicted me, rather than condemned me. A relationship with God is a raw, beautiful experience. It is something God so desperately wants everyone to have with Him. That is His ultimate priority for our lives. God will do whatever it takes to get your attention.

We all have the same access to God. He's been pursuing you your whole life. He is so patiently waiting for you to turn to Him so He can shower you with love, wrap you in grace, and teach you how to love yourself and others the way He intends us to.

"For every one of God's promises is 'Yes' in Him" (2 Corinthians 1:20).

God promises to give you strength.

xvii

God promises to give you peace.
God promises to give you hope.
God promises to give you wisdom.
God promises to give you eternal life.
God promises to never leave you.
God promises to always love you.
Every promise is a yes in Him.
You can take those promises to the bank. You can direct deposit them in your heart. God has made us thousands of promises, but they are promises you must claim over your life in order to experience the fullness of them.

Claiming His promises helps to build your faith. You can't just wake up one day and find faith. Faith is built by taking deliberate steps, making an intentional decision each day to pursue God. There will be times and seasons in our lives where our faith is shaken. There will be plenty of times in our lives where we get in a faith funk. Some days, our spiritual tank feels like it's on empty. Even the strongest believers in Christ have days where their faith feels weak.

That's how the building process works. That's how the journey with Jesus works. That's how faith and strength are built.

During those moments of weakness, we tend to feel guilty for losing our focus, from straying from God. But let me tell you something: Your weakness doesn't change the nature of Him. He is always faithful, and He is always ready to shine His face upon you with so much love, if you look to Him.

He wants you to know that being in His presence, and resting in His promises, is the only way for us to recharge. He is our power source, our spiritual fuel. We live in a busy, selfish world that has made it easy to forget that faith is built through stillness, rest, and dependence on Him. Society tells us to make time for self-care. God is telling you to make time for soul-care. He is never too far.

Sometimes, when I am going through tough seasons, I like to pick a Bible verse and claim it for that particular season. It's a verse I hold tight to and remind myself of. I remind myself that it's a promise that is true, and because I believe in God, then it for sure is a yes in Him. Write it on your bathroom mirror, write it in your planner, or save it as a lock screen on your phone. Put it somewhere that you can see it constantly and remind yourself of.

Here are two that I claimed as I began my journey through bowel reconstruction:

> Before healing the man born blind, Jesus said, "this happened so that God's works might be displayed in him." (John 9:3)

> Strength and honor are her clothing, and she can laugh at the time to come. (Proverbs 31:25)

These are promises I lean on and live by. I constantly remind myself of these promises. These verses make me feel like God is speaking to me every time I read them. I've claimed them like my life depends on it. These verses hold so much power, if you believe in the promise they hold. During that season of my life, I believed that God was healing me so I could glorify His power through it, and yes, I am strong, and I can have hope because He is my strength and my hope. I know how much this helped me, and I believe it will help you too.

We are only getting started.

Again, you have to claim His promises in order to receive them. Claiming a verse helps to give you hope, but it also teaches you to see how all of God's promises hold true. It helps to shape your perspective and learn about the character of Jesus.

God says to seek Him, and you will find Him; to knock and the door will be opened. That's a promise too.

The week I was preparing to schedule my last reconstructive surgery, I was surrounded with rainbows. In fact, I saw more rainbows during the year of my surgeries than I had in the last ten years. My week started off with a dream about rainbows. In my dream, I was driving my car, and I kept stopping the car to take pictures of all the rainbows I was seeing. A couple of nights after, I had the same exact dream. I was also reminded of the rainbow I saw before my previous surgery, and thankfully for Timehop, I was reminded of a rainbow I had seen on the same day, one year prior. I was trying to wrap my head around the revelation God was giving me; when I opened up my Bible that morning, I came across a verse in the book of John, which said, "This sickness will not end in death but it is for the glory of God, so that the Son of God may be glorified through it" (John 11:4).

With all the rainbows that surrounded me that week, and as I was preparing for my final surgery, I knew God was reminding me of what He promised. He promised me that He would restore my health during that season of my life, and He was showing me He is always with me, and always has been, holding my hand every step of the way.

The rainbow is a symbol of God's faithfulness and love. It is a beautiful reminder that God always keeps His word. Rest is always found in His promises.

In case you're wondering, God gave me a miracle. My sickness is gone. In 2019, God broke the chains of the prison my body had been in for so long. I am healed because of Him, and I understand now that God designs our battles and our pain to not only do the work in us to teach us to trust Him and be more dependent on Him, but to show others that His promises are real. God is real. Just as John said, things happen to us so that the work of God can be displayed in our lives. The end result of adversity is so God can get all the glory.

I don't know all the answers to life's questions, but I do know this: It took real pain to build a real faith.

When I look back on my trials and suffering, I can testify that the times I felt the strongest and most at peace were the times I clung tightest to God's promises. It's a peace that surpasses human understanding. If you're wondering how God wants to use you, look no further than your struggles. That is your story. The testimony comes after the test. The miracle is in our brokenness. God's power is perfected in our weakness, and that is how He turns our story of brokenness into one of redemption.

Let's continue to explore the power of leaning on God's promises and claiming them over your life. Faith is built through resting in Him. There is nothing in this world more powerful than a promise from God. From now on, let the rainbow be a reminder that just as God took care of Noah, He will also take care of you.

The proof is in the promise.

PART 1: ALIGNMENT

ACCEPTANCE, DISCIPLINE, AND TRANSFORMATION

Our spiritual growth, as believers in Christ, is structured around two very important things: what God wants to do *in* you, and what God wants to do *through* you.

God is more concerned about you than your surroundings and circumstances. A relationship with God is His single most important priority for your life. Part 1 of this book is solely focused on God's alignment in your life. When you align yourself with God's will, your new perspective on life allows you to see the world differently. It's a dynamic shift in thinking; it's a new perspective. It's a learning process that must take place, in order to truly embrace all of what God's promises have to offer you. Being aligned with His will enables Him to accomplish His will through you, as He transforms your heart and mind to be more like Him. This process allows you to understand the nature of God, as well as your true identity in Him.

The process of alignment can be broken down into three key lessons:

Acceptance: an understanding of what God says about who you are.

Discipline: a surrendering to His truths so He can cultivate your heart to be more like His.

Transformation: an awakening to believing that God has called you to a heavenly purpose.

CHAPTER 1
UNLEARNING

Part of learning about the nature of God, and who Jesus is, requires us to first unlearn some things about ourselves.

Unfortunately, we don't have to look very far to find our faults. Since the beginning of time, humanity has fallen to a broken, corrupt world that's tainted with sin. Sin is not something we can sugarcoat. We are all guilty of it. We all fall short, every single day. Human nature mixed with temptation is a recipe for disaster. It always has been. However, the Bible has made one thing very, very clear: God has had a plan for redemption since the beginning of humanity.

The Bible is filled with story after story after story about how God redeems His people. If you were to ask me to summarize the Bible in one sentence, I would put it to you like this: The Bible is God's love story.

The whole theme of the Bible is to show us God never gives up on us, and He has always loved us—and always will. We know that the ultimate price of redemption came at the cost of sacrificing His own Son to save His people. Jesus left the glories and riches of heaven to put on a mortal body and embrace the full weight and penalty of sin on Himself so we wouldn't have to.

A Terrible and Great Day

Think back to when Jesus died on the cross. I can't even begin to imagine how hopeless the people of Israel must have felt on that horrific day, which is what we now call Good Friday. Those who believed Jesus was their promised Savior were heartbroken that day. It represents the day Jesus gave His life to save the world. They didn't have a Bible to reference like we have, to tell them what was going to happen three days later. They had a living, breathing Savior walking among them, and they were able to witness and experience hope in mortal form. Their hope was literally tangible. And in Jesus's last moments, they watched their Savior, their hope, be murdered in the most torturous way possible. The world was dark, and people were full of pain, grief, and sorrow. Their hope was lost. But what people didn't realize then was that what they thought was the end of the world, the end of their hope, was actually the beginning of salvation. It was the beginning of hope. Jesus paid for all of us to have that gift. It cost Him everything; it cost us nothing.

The moments of pain were connected with His promises three days later, when Jesus conquered death and rose from the grave, fulfilling biblical prophecy.

I think we too often forget everything that happened the day Jesus died on the cross. We know He suffered the most excruciating death humanly possible, but it was so much more than a murder. It was so much deeper than we realize. Before Jesus died, He was mocked, beaten, ridiculed, spit on, cursed, and humiliated as he carried His cross up to Calvary. Keep in mind that even though He was Jesus, He was human. He wasn't exempt of any of the pain. There is no greater betrayal or injustice in history than that of Jesus's Crucifixion.

God poured His wrath out on Jesus that day. Jesus bore the full weight of all humanity's sin when He experienced the wrath of God while hanging on the cross. If you read the Old Testament, you know that God's wrath is not something to be taken lightly. Beyond that, Jesus had to experience the greatest moment of agony anyone could ever experience: total separation from God Himself. He not only had to suffer the physical pain, but He had to suffer the spiritual pain of being separated from His Father. Jesus had to experience wrath and abandonment so we would never have to. Even on our worst days and in our deepest valleys, we are never separated from God.

Ever.

One of the last things Jesus said on the cross was, "My God, my God, why have you forsaken me?" (Matthew 27:46).

Separation from God is hell, and there is nothing that could ever compare to the abandonment Jesus must have felt that day. For that reason, when you really understand the depth of the day Jesus was crucified, you can understand that you and I were both on His mind that day.

He gave His life to pay our ticket to heaven. Humanity was not worthy of a relationship with God, but He loved us so much that He had to make a way. His blood made us worthy. If it wasn't for His sacrifice, humanity would implode with self-destruction. Thankfully, we are called to a much different path in life.

Changing Our Perspective

So many of us still think of heaven with a works-based mentality—that is, if we do enough good or be good enough people, we will be worthy enough to be with Jesus in heaven. However, God already knew we would fall short. Your sins, faults, and shortcomings do not come as a turn-off to God. They also do not make Him love you any less. But the honest truth is, we are not worthy of everything heaven has to offer. Even on our best days, we are about as clean as a rag that's been drug through the mud and washed in the sewer. God is not looking for perfection. If perfection is what God wanted,

Jesus would have never had to come and live a perfect, sinless life to pay the cost for our sins.

We are allowed to change our perspective now, because of Him. Jesus is not nailed to a cross anymore. He conquered sin. He defeated death. Even though Jesus was removed from the cross and rose from the grave three days later, He left our sins hanging on the cross. Remember that when Jesus was put to death, our sins were put to death too. He broke the bondage of sin so we could have freedom, not as an excuse to sin but as a reason to follow the One Who made us worthy. He made it so easy for us to get to heaven; all we have to do is receive Him in our hearts, and eternity is ours.

I guess it's hard to believe that someone could love us that much, huh?

You see, there are two forces that are constantly fighting for your heart. It's important to understand that your soul has a very expensive price tag on it. There is a very real enemy of our souls that wants to rob you of that inheritance. The enemy (Satan) wants nothing more than to deter you from a relationship with Jesus. The enemy is so good at deceiving you into thinking that accepting Jesus's love, and accepting that gift of salvation, is supposed to be difficult. The reason the enemy makes it difficult is because his main motives of deterrence are accomplished through distraction, division, and feelings of guilt, fear, doubt, worry, shame, and anxiety. The enemy wants you to keep that works-based mentality because that makes it easier for him to convince you that you will never be good enough.

Jesus died so our identities can rest in Him and what He has done. The uncomfortable truth is that we really are not good enough. I am an unworthy sinner. You are too. It's something all humanity has in common. Like I said, God does not want or expect you to be perfect. But He does want you to understand that He is, and His grace covers all our imperfections. All He wants in exchange is a relationship with you.

When you open your heart to Jesus and decide to accept Him into your life, He is able to show you how to embrace His love, regardless of where you fall short and how many times you fall short. It's a love that He freely gives to anyone and everyone. It's a love that rescues you, a love that gives you eternal life, a love that empowers you and gives you confidence in knowing that you belong to an almighty King Who secured your citizenship in heaven through what He did on the cross. It is He Who tells you not to worry, be fearful, or wage war against one another. He tells us that we can have hope because He has already conquered evil. Your victory is secured the moment you place your faith in Him. You will cross the finish line when you step into heaven with Him for eternity.

Embracing God's promises first requires us to surrender to His truths. We must understand that we needed a perfect Savior to clean up our mess. We need to unlearn the works-based mentality that society has drilled into our brains and has fueled our success-driven work ethic. I think we sometimes feel we must try to prove our worth to God. You're not the only one if you've ever thought, *Once I get my life together, I'll get right with God.*

Believe it or not, that attitude alone can actually drive a wedge between you and your relationship with Him.

We are not capable of proving our worth to God. We are always going to fail. Don't let that discourage you. This is why we need His gift of grace and salvation. There is nothing we have to do except believe that Jesus came to this earth with one mission: to save the world. Just believing those words is the beginning of salvation. It's a simple truth that required a big sacrifice.

That's too easy, though, isn't it? We should have to do more to earn that heavenly inheritance, right?

That's what the enemy wants you to think. We will continue to dig into the enemy's motives throughout this book because I want to make sure you understand that God doesn't want you to be confused. God's voice is very clear when you allow His to be the loudest one in your life. The enemy wants to guilt us, shame us, and trick us into thinking heaven is too far away, and we have sinned too much to be worthy of redemption. The beautiful thing about Jesus is that we don't have to earn anything; He did it so we could have access to Him. Believing that truth allows you to truly embrace a relationship with Him. You are worth it to Him on your best days just as much as you are worth it to Him on your worst days.

> For you are saved by grace through faith, and this is not from yourselves; it is God's gift—not from works, so that no one can boast. (Ephesians 2:8–9)

Life is not about earning and deserving; it's about believing and receiving.

It's time to change our works-based mentality to a worth-based mentality.

The God of More Than Second Chances

The truth is, we need God's grace. We not only need to receive it, but we need to be changed by it. Through His grace, we are able to have faith, and faith is what we use to fill the gaps between our trials and our triumphs. Faith is what builds the bridge between earth and heaven. His grace sustains us, and our hope we have in Him is what elevates us to a higher purpose that is aligned with God's calling for our lives.

If you want a biblical example of an individual who embodied the need for God's grace, let me introduce you to a man named Paul. Paul was originally named Saul, before he had an encounter with Jesus that completely changed his life. In chapter 8 of the book of Acts, he was introduced as "Saul the Persecutor." Before he experienced Jesus, he had a reputation for being a very scary man. Seriously. He persecuted the church and sent death threats to those who followed Jesus. He threatened to imprison Jesus's disciples. For lack of better words, Saul was a spiritual terrorist. But when he truly experienced Jesus, it convicted him so much that he changed his name to Paul and spent the rest of his life following Him, writing letters to the churches, encouraging them in the faith, preaching the

Kingdom of God, and teaching others about Jesus Christ. In fact, Paul wrote half of the New Testament, which is a light source that many others use in following Jesus today.

Paul's story shows us that God, by the saving grace of Jesus Christ, is capable of transforming any human heart and using them to advance His Kingdom. Paul's story proves God can qualify anyone who is willing to be changed by His grace and answer their calling. Paul's story shows us we are never too far from God. It shows us that many of us feel unworthy of a second chance, but God gives us mercy every day. It is never too late to turn to Him and ask for another chance. In fact, He is the God of more than second chances. He really is that good.

Paul spent his life teaching others about Jesus because he knew the power of transformation that came through an experience which led to a relationship with Jesus. God used Paul's story to illustrate His power. That's what the Lord meant when He told Paul, "My grace is sufficient for you, for my power is perfected in weakness" (2 Corinthians 12:9).

One last thing to help put Paul's story in perspective for you.

Sometimes, I wake up early enough to catch the sunrise. Other times, I catch the sky at the perfect time right before sunset. The way the sun breaks the night into dawn and the way it sets on the horizon puts off the most beautiful colors.

I know you know what I'm talking about. There's the deep orange, pink, and sometimes purple colors, and the clouds just add this undeniable texture to the sky that make it so incredibly captivating. Well, I'm that girl who is always trying to take the perfect picture of the sky so I can capture just how beautiful it is. My camera roll is filled with hundreds of pictures of the sky. But it doesn't matter how hard I try, or how many pictures I take, the pictures just never do it justice. The pictures are never as beautiful as actually seeing the sky in person.

The same thing goes for Jesus.

Paul, myself, and many others can sit here and explain what a relationship with Jesus looks like, describe what He has done for us and for the world, and try to paint the picture of the beauty of a relationship with Him, but a relationship with Jesus is not something that can be explained; it can only be experienced. I say that because we are all in this world to discover how to journey through life with Jesus and unwrap the treasures of His promises, as well as discovering our true identity, purpose, and calling He has had for us since before we were born. Your life is a miracle, and your story is a testimony of God's power and grace. He designed your life in such a way to illustrate His strength and allow Him to shine through you.

You are a unique expression of God, and He wants nothing more than for you to find faith and confidence in Him so you can see the beauty of the picture He is painting for your life. Once you understand the nature and goodness of God, you will want to spend the rest of your life telling the world Who paints the skies and how your testimony is God's redemptive masterpiece.

CHAPTER 2
BACK TO THE BASICS

Before we dive any further, I believe it is important to take a moment to break some barriers regarding the complexity of Jesus, as well as the Bible itself. If I had a dollar for every time I've heard someone say the Bible is too hard to understand, I'd be rich. Somewhere along the line of our ancestors, we've strayed from the true simplicity that is found in Jesus Christ. If you find yourself having a hard time reading the Bible, then you, my friend, are in the right place.

Keep reading.

We were not given scripture for us to be confused. The Bible is not supposed to be a mystery to those who have stepped into a relationship with Him. The Bible is the user manual of life. It contains everything we will ever need to know. It helps us makes sense of the confusion going on in this world. But there are some key points that are worth mentioning in order to grasp the nature of the Bible and why it was written. I believe that understanding this is key to not only uncovering its treasures, but also finding enjoyment in reading its rich, powerful stories.

Old versus New

First things first: It is absolutely crucial to find a Bible with your preferred translation. There are many different translations available for you to read; your preference is completely up to you. If reading the Bible is a new journey for you, I would suggest starting with the Christian Standard Bible (CSB) or the New English Translation (NET). Or, if thy shall prefer thou Word otherwise, you can try the King James Version (KJV). It's completely up to you.

As you probably already know, the Bible is separated into two parts: the Old Testament and the New Testament.

Think of the Old Testament as a history book of Israel, as well as the personal narratives of individuals living in those times. The Old Testament is full of stories of leaders and prophets whose hearts were tuned into hearing from God. These leaders and prophets also made up the majority of authors in that part of the Bible. More importantly, they were people, just like you and me, who had a desire to seek and understand God's heart and will. These stories tell what it looked like when people chose not to follow God, but it is also full of stories of what it looked like to bring real pain and suffering to God for restoration. They are stories of how God uses the most imperfect people to accomplish His plans. They are stories that show us the true nature of God. He always redeems His people when they turn to Him; He longs to forgive His people and has always been gracious to welcome new beginnings. They are stories of how God used adversity to train His people to trust Him, as well as prophets who had a heart that desired to navigate people to God.

The stories and books that make up the Old Testament include prophecies that were fulfilled in the New Testament or will soon be fulfilled in the days before Jesus Christ's Second Coming. In short, the Old Testament predicts the coming of the Messiah (Jesus Christ), and the New Testament reveals the Messiah.

The character of the Old Testament (the old covenant/promise) was based on continuous offerings made by the people to the priest, who would go before God to make atonement for people's sins.

God instituted this sacrificial system, under the Law of Moses, to demonstrate the need for righteousness. We had to first understand the law in order to understand the need for grace and for forgiveness of our sins. The character of the New Testament (the new covenant/promise) is based on the one and only sacrifice needed to pay for those sins, past, present, and future. Remember, God has had a plan for redemption all along. We see in the Old Testament that we were never capable of righteousness; sin has always corrupted this effort. Jesus made the way and gave us a new commandment to live by and a new way of living, unshackled by sin.

The New Testament is really as simple as this:

The first four books (Matthew, Mark, Luke, and John) are eyewitness accounts of Jesus's life on earth during His ministry. They are full of Jesus's teachings and miracles. The last words Jesus spoke to His disciples, after He rose from the dead and before He ascended into heaven, were, "Go, therefore, and make disciples of all nations ... teaching them to observe everything I have commanded you. And remember, I am with you always, to the end of the age" (Matthew 28:19–20).

The rest of the books (Acts to Revelation) are letters to people and churches as a result of Jesus's Great Commission. What you are reading in the New Testament is how the movement of Christianity began. Those letters (written by Paul and several others) are our reminders and encouragement to keep our faith in God, as well as instructions on how to maintain a productive spiritual life.

Jesus left His disciples, as well as the rest of the world, a new promise/commandment. His disciple, John, recorded these instructions the day before Jesus would be crucified. Jesus said, "I give you a new command: Love one another. Just as I have loved you, you are also to love one another. By this everyone will know that you are my disciples, if you love one another" (John 13:34–35).

Jesus's disciples started the church. They started the movement of Christianity.

Listen, please do not get caught up on fitting Christianity into a religious box. Too many people have been misinformed and hurt because of this. In fact, those who persecuted and crucified Jesus were among the so-called "religious." Society has made Christianity way too complicated when it is not necessary. Paul reminds us in his letters (half of the New Testament) that Jesus always kept it simple. He reminds us that the church is not a building or a religion; it is the people.

Let me explain it this way:

I call myself an American, because I live in America. Makes sense, right?

For this same reason, we call ourselves Christians, not because we identify with a religion, but because Christ lives in us. The Holy Spirit resides in our hearts. Christianity is all about relationship. When we invite Jesus into our lives, we are simultaneously allowing His Spirit to dwell in our hearts. That is what gives us the insight to uncover and understand the treasures of God's words and promises, as well as the power for us to be courageous in telling people the good news of the Gospel. The invitation to a relationship with Jesus is a prerequisite for radical transformation in our hearts.

Extension of the Commission

The Bible's first generation of disciples understood this very well. The letters of the New Testament can be interpreted as our encouragement to pursue Jesus, since His sacrifice made us worthy to enter the Pearly Gates of heaven. You and I are also called to be disciples. Scripture may have been written thousands of years ago, but the Bible is timeless; it is so relevant to believers today.

You can consider my entire book as a letter to you. We are here to build one another up in the faith and knowledge of Jesus Christ and what He did for this world. Our work here is an extension of the Great Commission, to continue to help change hearts and advance the Kingdom of God. I am writing this book for the simple fact that my life has been forever changed by the transformational and redeeming power of His love, and that's something I desperately desire for everyone to experience. I want others to understand the simplicity in Christ, our heavenly mission, and to answer the calling of discipleship as well. We are all called to be ambassadors of God.

Another way to grasp the perspective of Jesus and his teachings is knowing He always spoke and taught in parables. Parables are earthly stories with heavenly meanings. His preaching in parables was a fulfillment of prophecy, and Jesus used parables to open our eyes to deeper insight into Him and give us a glimpse into the spiritual realm to convey His truths to us. He did this because those who are not open to truth will be confused; they will not understand. But those who have a heart willing to open and ears willing to listen to His truths will be able to fully fathom their meaning.

Paul explained it like this: "For the word of the cross is foolishness to those who are perishing, but it is the power of God to us who are being saved" (1 Corinthians 1:18).

There are and will continue to be many people who stumble over the simplicity of Christ. I will say that this is not entirely their fault. If we are getting back to the basics, and if we want to be the people who advance Jesus's heavenly mission, we must understand that the nature of God's grace is meant to serve as an extension of the same grace He showed all of us on the cross. Many times, we forget that the only way some people learn about Jesus is through how they are treated by others, and then we Christians wonder why people have a foul sense of who Jesus is. Some people who have yet to find Jesus won't be able to see what His grace looks like until they are treated with grace. When Jesus was asked to settle an argument about the most important commandment, He responded with a very bold, yet simple truth. It doesn't get any simpler than this:

> Love the Lord your God with all your heart, with all your soul, with all your mind, and with all your strength. The second is, love your neighbor as yourself. There is no command greater than these. (Mark 12:30–31)

We are supposed to love, without reciprocity—because that is how Jesus loved.

The truth is, I don't want to know how many times I've offended God. He could probably fill the rest of these pages with a list of my offenses and sins, plus some. Do you know how many times you've offended God? Do you know how many times we have sinned? But how did God respond? How does He always respond?

By loving us through our mistakes and our flaws. His grace does not give us an excuse to sin, but instead gives us a reason to pursue Him because of His never-ending mercy and forgiveness. The fact that God doesn't count our transgressions or hold our offenses against us should directly impact the way we respond to offenses by others. God has always decided that love wins. We must also hold the same, permanent disposition. God has an answer in all of His promises, no matter how many times we've fallen short and offended Him.

Love is a big part of our heavenly mission, to win hearts and help people navigate their way to heaven. It is our job to show the world what it looks like to be wrapped in the grace we call our salvation; that type of grace is what changes the world.

But here's the thing: We can't bully people into finding Jesus, and we most definitely can't love and forgive others with the exception of those who offend us, disagree with us, or dislike us. That's not what the nature of God's grace represents. When discussing the current issues in today's world, I've heard many people say, "You can't just love and light your way through it."

Yes, you can.

As a matter of fact, that's exactly what we are supposed to do. Love is the most powerful force on the planet. Love is what kept Jesus on the cross the day He sacrificed Himself for our sins. Allow me to reiterate the simplicity that we have in Christ. When I talk about the word *love*, I'm not comparing it to an emotional, sentimental outpouring or expression. Love is a force. Love is the only force capable of transforming an enemy into a friend. Love is a force because it transforms with redemptive power. Love convicts. Love creates understanding. Love creates the capacity to forgive. Jesus built His entire Kingdom on the foundation of love.

And guess what?

To this day, millions of people have died for Him. There is no experience you will find in this world that helps you understand the power of love than experiencing a relationship with Him.

His love and light are bright enough to illuminate this entire world. I know this because the Bible says that when Jesus comes back to reclaim His Kingdom, His Second Coming, He is bringing a new heaven and earth with Him. It says that there will be no darkness but there will also be no sun, because the glory of His light will be bright enough to illuminate His entire Kingdom. As we look through the lens of love and grace as it relates to His simplicity, let's ask ourselves these questions:

How many sunrises do we have to witness to understand that God's mercies are new every morning?

How many times do the birds have to chirp for us to see that even the animals sing God's praises?

How many times must we suffer before we learn to embrace peace, resting in the fact that God fights for us?

How many times does Jesus have to (theoretically) die on a cross for us to understand that His one sacrifice was enough to make us worthy in the sight of God?

How many times must we be reminded that true hope is found in the fact that those who believe in Him have a whole eternity in heaven to look forward to?

I don't know how many times it will take, but I plan to spend the rest of my life reminding others of the true and wonderful simplicity we have in Christ. I hope along the way, I can encourage others to join me in doing the same. Even the apostle Paul spent his ministry reminding people of this true and simple fact. Jesus broke the chains from the bondage of sin, which means we can change our perspective and spend our energy focusing on living life under His crown, instead of polishing and bejeweling our own.

> Set your mind on things above, not earthly things.
> (Colossians 3:2)

We are citizens of heaven before we are citizens of this earth. It is our obligation to show others what grace and love look like, to stand in the middle of the offenses and for people who are hurting and show up with compassion and not condemnation. We must stand in the middle and absorb the tensions of this world with grace, truth, and light. As followers of Christ, we must be comfortable with being uncomfortable, stand in the tensions of society, and act as the filter for deciphering the harsh realities of this world and transforming them into purpose, life-giving truths, and direction. And while we stand in the middle, we should be the filter and the lens, to magnify Jesus in everything we do as well as magnifying His promises when the enemy puts in overtime in attempting to deceive people and deter them from a relationship with Jesus.

God rewards those who seek Him, and He also reveals the treasures of His promises as long as His children are willing to listen. Thankfully, He is patient with us. Our instructions are simple. Our commandment is to love.

It's time to get back to the basics.

CHAPTER 3
IDENTITY CRISIS

It is impossible for us to love ourselves, and to love others the way God wants us to, if we don't understand how much we are loved by Him first. If no one has ever told you this, let me be the first:

You are immeasurably loved and treasured by the One Who sits on the throne in heaven.

Whether you know it or not, God has been pursuing you your whole life. However, we live in a fast-paced society, where culture and status hold a lot of the weight in how we define our identity. It often seems that we allow society to put labels on our identity, which is how many people form opinions and beliefs about others. The problem is, the things that define us are often the things that divide us. A few examples of this are race, ethnicity, religion, and political party. Our true identity lies in the fact that we are all sons and daughters, and brothers and sisters, who were created by an Almighty Father in heaven, and He is the only one allowed to define who we are.

Society, on the other hand, instructs us to shape our identity contradictory to how God has already defined us. This world has developed an identity crisis, because there are two opposing forces who tell us how to discover our true identity. Spoiler alert: society is wrong.

The world tells us to love ourselves, but scripture tells us to "love God with all of your heart, soul and mind" (Matthew 22:37).

The world tells us to follow our heart, but Jesus said, "Follow me" (Matthew 16:24).

The world tells us to believe in ourselves, but God tells us to believe in Him (John 14:1).

The world tells us to speak our truth, but God says, "I am the truth" (John 14:6).

The world tells us to take pride in who we are, but scripture tells us that God hates pride (Proverbs 8:13).

The world tells us that we should discover ourselves, but Jesus said to "deny yourself" (Matthew 16:24).

Before we rest in any of God's promises, we must first rest in where our identity comes from and Who it is tied to. After reading the first chapter of this book, you know He tells us we are worthy enough for Him to bear the burden of all of our sin, and He gave His life so we could understand just how much we are loved.

> For God loved the world in this way: He gave his one and only Son, so that everyone who believes in him will not perish but have eternal life. For God did not send his Son into the world to condemn the world, but to save the world through him. (John 3:16–17)

First Steps

One of the most important things about our understanding and the pursuit of our purpose is that we must first understand where our identity comes from, which all begins with relationship and learning to see yourself the way God sees you. Everyone is looking for purpose, but in trying to find our purpose in life, we are skipping a very important step many of us forget to work on (some neglect it entirely). We do not take the time to learn our true identity. Our identity stems deeper than just being a child of God. As a child of God, you have a Holy Spirit living inside of you. You are a complex yet beautiful creation made in God's image.

The beginning of God's alignment of our lives to His will and receiving His promises involves cultivating a humble heart that recognizes a need for Him. God intentionally made us with a missing piece of our heart that only He can fill. That is why we often feel lacking or unsatisfied, no matter how much we accomplish or how "successful" we are. I put that word in quotations because if you think about it, success is often determined by societal standards as well. Success is derived by a continuous acquisition of materials and accomplishments. That is why no matter how hard the world tries or accomplishes, we always want more. God calls us to live a life defined by significance and meaning, which can only be accomplished by the heavenly works He has put in our hearts. It is not until we receive His grace and love, and surrender our lives to Him, that we realize He is everything we need, and the only One Who can truly bring unity to a world that continues to be divided by status quo and labels.

God never stops pouring into us. He fills us with love and grace when we allow Him to reside in our hearts, but He doesn't stop there. He knows that once we allow Him to pour into us, once we surrender to His sovereign, patient, gracious discipline about who He says He is and what He says about who we are, our cup will begin to overflow. With that overflow, we begin to understand what God is manifesting inside of us, to bring to the world the best version of ourselves. This is so that others will be led to Him. We will talk about this manifestation in part 2 of this book, but understand that while you are learning and aligning and embracing spiritual discipline and maturity, God is stirring up an incredible work in you that He is preparing to share with the world.

The Importance of Surrender

For the longest time, the word *surrender* scared me. It made me super uncomfortable. If I had realized back then that surrender would result in freedom, I would have done it years ago. A lot of people think that surrendering your life to Jesus means completely uprooting your life. In a sense, it actually does. But making the choice to surrender your life to Him means that you're ready to start a building process in your heart and your life. It means making a choice to be intentional in your pursuit of Jesus every day.

It's a surrender of your will, to learning more about His will.

It's a surrender of old thoughts about who you once were.

It's a surrender of giving up the thought that you have to work harder to earn His favor.

Surrendering allows you to willingly engage in the process of spending alone time with God, to allow Him to pull out some of the weeds in your heart, so He can plant seeds of His promises so that His truths can take root and grow.

God's ultimate goal through a relationship with Him is to transform our minds and hearts to be more like His. He gave us the gift of grace so we could be transformed by it and be examples to others of what grace looks like.

Part of understanding your true identity is reminding yourself of the two forces that are constantly battling for your heart. One of the most valuable lessons we could ever learn is that the enemy does his best work in the depth of uncertain minds.

Read that one more time.

You see, God and the enemy use our trials in life for the exact same purpose: to get into our hearts. The difference is, God moves in our hearts to build faith, while the enemy moves to build fear. Satan uses feelings of doubt, worry, anxiety, and fear to make even more fogginess out of our uncertain circumstances, so he can distract us from a relationship with God. Understanding this is what will keep your mind and heart guarded when those familiar emotions surface in your mind.

Don't forget, the enemy loves to remind you of your past. That's his favorite pastime (pun intended). Reminders of our past are nothing we can escape; we can't change the past, and the enemy knows this. Let me give you a promise you can practice the next time the enemy wants to creep up on you and say "Remember when …":

> Therefore, if anyone is in Christ, he is a new creation; the old has passed away, and see, the new has come! Everything is from God, who has reconciled us to himself through Christ and has given us the ministry of reconciliation. That is, in Christ, God was reconciling the world to himself, not counting their trespasses against them, and he has committed the message of reconciliation to us. (2 Corinthians 5:17–19)

God is the Father of forgiveness. He doesn't hold anything against you. Your sin, your past, your mistakes do not change God's faithfulness, and they never will. Even the mistakes you haven't made yet are forgiven, when you are in Christ and ask for forgiveness. There is nothing you can do that would ever make God love you any less. For every lie the enemy throws at you, there's a promise of God that you can always use as your rebuttal. Even the enemy knows the power of God's promises.

The Enemy Exposed

The enemy is here to dim your light and extinguish your God-ignited flame by any means necessary. I'm going to let you in on a little secret: When you understand what God says about who you are, the source of your light, and the power of your fire, you are unstoppable, and the devil knows it. You are a force when you strap yourself with the Word of God. The enemy hates it. He hates it because he knows God's authority can never be overruled. God's authority is sovereign and superior. And you, my friend, are allowed to walk confidently in the shadow of this authority.

The Bible reminds us to be alert: "Your adversary the devil is prowling around like a roaring lion, looking for anyone he can devour" (1 Peter 5:8).

Learn this lesson from the animal kingdom: When the lion is looking for its next meal in the wild, who does it usually target?

The weak one. The injured one. The one who has gotten distracted and fallen away from its herd, or the baby who strays from the rest of the family. We've all seen how this plays out on *National Geographic*. They look for the easy targets, the most vulnerable, or the ones who are lacking protection. Lions go in for the kill when they see their opportunity.

The enemy feels the same way about the children of God. He targets those who have fallen away from a relationship with God; those who are most vulnerable to falling into his lie trap; those who have yet to step into a relationship with Jesus Christ. He will even target God's strongest warriors, the moment they let their guard down. The devil prowls around, waiting for his opportunity to sink his claws into our hearts.

The enemy's main weapon is disunity. He will use our own circumstances and emotions as bait, to deceive us, and will even try to play us with our own sin; he'll do whatever it takes to shift our focus from God and drive a wedge between us and spending time with God. So when we see people at each other's throats, divided on issues, or succumbing to feelings of shame, fear, worry, or doubt, the enemy is doing exactly what he wants. He's claiming that victory.

Through discipline of God's truths, we know now that we have the authority from God to refuse to give the enemy that power in our lives. Never let yourself forget that you are a child of a King, and because of that, you have the victory.

When we soak ourselves in God's presence, and focus on what He wants to teach us, especially when it comes to our identity, we can recognize the enemy's motives and schemes. God teaches us how to identify ways of thinking that are not His. We can bring those emotions to Him so He can use His promises to remind us that in Him, we have armor; we have strength. We can recognize the battle for what it is. It's a battle of God's truths versus the enemy's lies. At the end of the day, you realize the enemy is just a big, loud, noisy chatterbox.

Your mind is a very powerful, underutilized tool. The mind will believe whatever you feed it. The most effective skill we can learn is how to identify ways of thinking that are not from God, so we can know which ones we should be feeding our heart, and which thoughts we should be taking captive and drop-kicking out of our mind, so they don't have the opportunity to take root in our heart and take hold of us.

Imagine it like this: Every thought that is positive or uplifting, that encourages you to be strong, or any scripture you read in the Bible should be planted like a seed. Those seeds should be cared for, watered, and allowed to take root in your heart so you can grow and blossom into the beautiful, strong person God created you to be. On the flip side, whatever thoughts bring you anxiety, fear, worry, or discouragement, and your negative self-talk, should be pulled up and thrown out like a weed, before they begin to take root. Simply put, those thoughts are not from God.

Discerning God's truths from the enemy's lies is an important skill to learn. It's a skill the enemy does not want you to know about.

In nature, weeds suck up a lot of water, which is needed in order for the neighboring plants and flowers to grow. Weeds will destroy a garden if they're not pulled up before they're matured. The same principle applies to your heart. Water the seeds, pluck the weeds.

Let me plant a seed in your heart now: "In all these things, we are more than conquerors through him who loved us" (Romans 8:37).

I could write a whole chapter on this verse alone.

God calls us conquerors?

Yes, that promise is yours to claim, as long as you choose to let

God's voice (His promises) be the loudest one in your life. Plant it. Write it on your bathroom mirror. Look at it every single day. Remind yourself that what God says about you holds so much more weight than the enemy's manipulative lies and calculated distractions. I don't know who needs to hear this right now, but the spirit of fear, the spirit of depression, and the spirit of doubt are not your thoughts; they are all products of the enemy's loud and obnoxious voice and motives.

The more time you spend with God in His Word, the easier it will be to understand which voice is for you and which voice is against you. With this time spent, you become more familiar with and receptive to the voice of conviction, and less responsive to the voice of condemnation. Let me remind you again that there is absolutely no condemnation in Jesus. Jesus said it Himself; plant it:

> For God did not send his Son into the world to condemn the world, but to save the world through him. (John 3:17)

God is for you; He fights for you. The same spirit that lifted Christ from the dead, lives within you. He calls me and you conquerors, because if you receive the gift of salvation and invite Him into your life, then you can rest in the fact that Jesus already has the victory. We truly have no idea the strength and power of what God can do in us, for us, and through us. This type of strength is found through resting in Him. His promises not only shape our identity, but are the source of our strength. God has equipped us to live beyond our natural strength, by depending on Him and Him alone. He goes before us, is behind us, and is beside us. His strength is out of this world.

Literally.

No matter how strong we are in our faith, those negative feelings and emotions are always going to visit. No one is exempt. We are given a spirit of power, love, and a sound mind, but that does not mean we can eradicate fear. The enemy is always going to make jabs at us with his fear spear. But the point is to not let those feelings take up residence in your heart. There's a difference between an emotion being a visitor and becoming a resident. Through taking hold of the Lord's promises over the enemy's lies, you are able to defend yourself with the Word of God. God does not want us to be fearful, because fear is what blocks us from allowing His strength to be what engages our attitudes and efforts, to be bold and confident in trusting Him. Fear has no place here. You can cling to God's truths and take the enemy's lies captive because as a child of God, you are equipped with that power.

The Bible is our battle weapon. The life we live is spiritual warfare.

Even Jesus used the Word of God as His defense. He was not exempt from temptation. When He was tempted in the wilderness after fasting for forty days, the enemy, knowing He was hungry and exhausted, came creeping up with his trickery. For every deceptive attempt the devil tried to make, Jesus responded with,

"It is written."

"It is written."

"It is written."

Jesus responded with the Word of God. Every time.

> Then Jesus told him, "Go away, Satan! For it is written: Worship the Lord your God, and serve only him." Then the devil left him and angels came and began to serve him. (Matthew 4:10–11)

Silly, little Satan. I hope you can see how Jesus set the example of the power of God's promises.

God hasn't forgot about you or your prayers. There are seasons of our lives where we feel that God is far from us, but that couldn't be further from the truth. God is always working to buff out the areas of your heart where you can replace question with confidence.

God uses some of the darkest, most difficult moments of our lives to break the barriers in our heart that have been built with fear, anxiety, and doubt. Things might seem uncertain, but His plan is not. God is always trying to lovingly remind us that He is in control.

Some things happen to us as a consequence of sin, and a lot of times, things happen to people who don't deserve it. As children of God, we are never victims of our circumstances. If you always have that victim mindset, you are always going to feel defeated. This is where we must remind ourselves that surrender is key. Even when we might not feel that God is good, we can still rest in this promise:

> We know that all things work together for the good of those who love God, who are called according to his purpose. (Romans 8:28)

God isn't in the business of making you feel comfortable. I know that sounds completely contradictory to everything I've said so far, but hear me out. Living a life surrendered to Christ means living outside your comfort zone a lot. He lovingly disciplines us, but we have to be humble enough to be willing to sit through the discomfort of what God wants to teach us. Learning our identity in Christ is a heavy, convicting process. But this process comes with growth, and with growth comes transformation. That is when you can truly discover the beauty of what a relationship with God is all about and start to better understand all He has created you to be. That is the beginning of God's alignment of His character and will in your heart and in your life.

Living for Him and resting in His promises give you the strength to, in the words of the apostle Paul, "fight the good fight." God is more concerned about what He is doing in you than the circumstance you are going through. That's how we grow in our faith, grow in spiritual maturity, and grow to know Jesus's character. That's how we learn what God truly wants to teach us about ourselves. Growth and transformation can only occur outside our comfort zones. After all, plants can't grow without a little rain.

Don't let the weeds of uncertainty distract you from the flowers God is planting in your life. I encourage you to take hold of God's hand, and He will take hold of your heart. There is no greater power or joy than discovering your true identity and strength in Jesus Christ.

The King of Kintsugi

On June 19, 2019, I had my second reconstructive bowel surgery; my large intestine was removed. One night, as I was lying in my hospital bed, I took some time to reflect on everything that had happened since the beginning of that year. I looked down at my stomach to see a three-inch scar from my previous surgery, a new three-inch incision from the most recent surgery, surgery tape, a drain tube, bruising, and a new stoma (opening to an ileostomy bag). To paint the picture, I was quite the surgical work of art. Reflecting even further, my body felt like one big bruise since the first surgery, four months prior. I still had one more surgery left, to complete the bowel reconstruction.

I often referred to my surgeries as the "reconstructive rodeo," simply because of the physical and mental challenges that paired with the roller-coaster ride of the trauma I repeatedly put my body through. As soon as I finally felt myself regaining strength from one surgery, I was knocked back down by the next one. As I was lying in the hospital, I may have looked like a broken mess, but I did not feel like one.

It amazes me how incredibly resilient the human body is. Even for those with a diseased immune system like mine, our bodies are always fighting to heal themselves, no matter what scale of trauma it goes through. With the help of science, we are able to manipulate our bodies so they can function without certain organs, as a means to restore the body.

With the help of God, He enables us to see and experience the beauty in the broken in the midst of our healing and restoration.

We've all been broken in some way, shape, or form. We live with physical scars or emotional scars—or both. Every one of us needs physical healing, emotional healing, or spiritual healing. We live in a world full of broken minds, hearts, spirits, bodies, and relationships. We live in a broken world with people who enjoy doing the breaking, and with people who are at the other end of brokenness. Healing is something God is fully equipped to handle, if we surrender our broken pieces to Him.

If you didn't know, Kintsugi is a Japanese art that takes broken pieces of pottery and uses liquid gold as an adhesive to reattach the ceramic pieces. In Japanese, the word means "golden repair." Using gold in the cracks of the pieces strengthens the piece while making it even more beautiful and unique. Kintsugi is a way to recognize and admire the beauty of broken pieces.

What's even more unique is the chemical makeup of gold. Gold is not only precious because of its monetary and aesthetic value, but it is an incredibly durable and malleable element. It's also one of the only chemical elements on the periodic table that does not react with any other element. In other words, gold is pretty tough.

Brokenness is required for us to become stronger. True strength is manifested in our times of weakness. Brokenness can sometimes happen instantly, but growth and healing does not. I'm sure you've heard the phrase, "trust the process." You should know that the art of Kintsugi is a very elaborate, time-consuming process. But for those who treasure their ceramic pieces, it's worth it. The meaning behind this type of artwork is that although the cracks are noticeable, and it is not restored to its original form, the restored product is embraced and appreciated in its own unique beauty.

That's how God feels about you and me.

Without God, we place the burden on ourselves to heal our physical and emotional traumas. We use our own glue to hold our broken pieces in place. I don't know about you, but that is a strength I have never been able to find on my own. It simply doesn't exist.

God wants you to come to Him as you are, but He doesn't want you to stay that way. In fact, He knows that once we make the decision to come to Him, we will never be the same—and that's the whole point. The time it takes to put your pieces back together is worth it to Him, because what He is teaching you in the midst of construction, or reconstruction, is very valuable. God is very patient with us. He wants to show us that although we experience brokenness, it does not define us. As a matter of fact, brokenness is precious to Him, because it makes us vulnerable, and sometimes vulnerability is the only way we allow God to get into our hearts. There is beauty in broken because He is the only One Who can put our broken pieces back together with something stronger and more beautiful. It's that little-big thing called grace. His grace is our golden glue, which allows us to appreciate our broken pieces, knowing He is using those pieces to turn our brokenness into a story of redemption. What we learn in the midst of our brokenness and adversity is the metaphorical gold that God is using to piece us back together; and it comes with learning exactly what is molding us into a better version of ourselves along the way. There's nothing like the grace of God.

Although you never forget the pain of brokenness, in the end, you can appreciate the lessons learned and the beauty in your broken pieces. Even after they're broken, God—if we allow Him—always seems to find a way to put them right back together. It might not look the same, but it makes for an inspiring testimony.

After all, what Jesus has already done for us is so much bigger than anything that could ever happen to us. The trials and brokenness we experience are the catalyst for spiritual strength and wisdom. God must discipline us before we can understand how to use our pain as the platform to illustrate our testimony and showcase the Lord's glory.

The scars on my stomach will always remind me who the King

of Kintsugi is. I'm not the same person I was before I experienced the physical brokenness of chronic illness, but the process of healing and the lessons learned along the way have been worth the time it took to understand what God was trying to teach me in the midst of brokenness. My prayer for you is that you always remember that pain and adversity are absolutely necessary for God to accomplish His purpose in us. Not because God wants to see you suffer, but because He needs you to understand that He is completely capable of handling your battle; it was already His in the first place. His purpose for you, for me, and for this world is so big that even if He were to tell us His plans, we wouldn't be able to fully fathom His dominion. Getting through our times of adversity will inevitably include hardship, challenges, and a testing of your faith. But on the other side of pain is healing, a deeper-rooted faith, and a greater understanding of God's sovereignty and kindness. Day by day, through each step of faith to get to know Him on a much deeper level, He is transforming you as you allow Him to plant His promises in your heart.

The Beauty in Broken

Have you ever thought that maybe God designs our problems so He can use us to demonstrate His power? Let this be your reminder that we serve a God Who has a reputation for bringing miracles out of the impossible. Your pain is His platform to work some serious miracles in your life. A lot of times, we are tempted into feeling like the victim of our circumstances, because things happen to us that we don't deserve. A lot of bad things happen to good people, and we are put into situations that were not a result of sin. Some things are just out of our control. But that's not the lens through which we should dissect the meaning behind adversity. For example, Jesus did not deserve to be beaten, tortured, and murdered, but He endured the suffering because He knew that in the end, it would result in ultimate good: His glory and our salvation.

Every problem can be worked out for good in our lives, but only to the extent that we are willing to trust Him. Those same problems can become roadblocks in our lives, when we react with distrust and approach them with a victim mentality. The key is choosing how we respond to our problems.

What you will see is that when you continue to trust God through difficulty and hardship, and take steps of faith anyway, you learn He truly is with you every step of the way. God is working out His good, perfect plan in ways you aren't even aware of. Everything about your life plays a role in God's Kingdom. You must choose to trust Him, even when it is hard, and even when you are in the darkest tunnel with no light in sight.

That is exactly why God tells us to walk by faith, not by sight.

We enable ourselves to walk by faith when we choose to fill our mind with His presence, instead of our problems. It is not an easy thing to do, which is why it's a choice we must continue to make every day. If you're like me, it's a choice I have to make multiple times a day.

Whatever season you are in, God is working through you so you can grow into a deeper relationship with Him. He wants this deep relationship with you so you can come alongside others who are in search of faith for their fight. He wants you to trust Him so you can receive all the blessings He promises through faithfulness and obedience. The reason we stay frustrated with our problems is because we don't give God full control and trust Him to deliver us from those problems. We tend to spend more time focusing on our problems, rather than His promises. When you focus on your problems, you tend to look through the lens of adversity as a victim, but when you focus on His promises, you have no other choice but to look through the lens of adversity as a victor, a conqueror.

Brokenness does not disqualify us from God using us. In fact, it is from our broken places that God ignites the fiery passion to serve our purpose, all while getting back on our feet. That is how He uses us to help rescue others. It is crucial for us to embrace all the valleys we walk through in life and allow God to show us the incredible strength and beauty that are to be revealed, no matter what brokenness we may face.

Sometimes, God has to break you before He can build you. The miracle is in the breaking. Embrace the lessons. Your scars are gold, remember that.

CHAPTER 4
STUDYING FOR A TEST YOU'VE ALREADY PASSED

Once you've learned the basic math of 1 Savior + 3 nails = 4given, you've passed the ultimate test. Let me rephrase: Jesus Christ passed the test for you; He's given you an A+. You get to run through the gates of heaven with flying colors when you confess with your mouth and believe in your heart that Jesus is your Savior.

However, this is just the beginning.

> Then Jesus said to his disciples, "If anyone wants to follow after me, let him deny himself, take up his cross, and follow me." (Matthew 16:24)

Many people falsely assume that once they start a relationship with Jesus, life gets easier. I wish I could say that was true, but the truth is, it doesn't get easier; you just get stronger. Your strength is being built when you are choosing to walk by faith, trusting in the promises that God has given you, learning to discern the voice of the Holy Spirit, and being guided by it.

Changing Direction

When you accept Jesus into your life and begin a relationship with Him, you are making the decision to pursue righteousness, all while still living in a world full of sin. You can either follow the world, or you can follow Jesus, but you can't do both. As you spend more time alone with Jesus, and in scripture, you will find yourself being tempted and convicted at the same time. Remember, there are two forces battling for your control of your heart and mind.

When you decide to pursue Jesus and allow His truths to discipline you, you begin to function with a much higher level of thinking and conviction. You are more conscientious of when you sin. As you learn more, you see more. You see that this walk with Jesus is actually graciously nudging you in the opposite direction as the rest of the world. This is a good thing. I would be doing you a disservice if I told you this faith journey is a cakewalk for Christians, but please do not confuse discomfort with unhappiness.

As you spend more time with God, and meditate and sit in His presence through prayer, or by reading scripture, your heart begins to open more and more, and that is when He is able to pour revelations of His truth and promises into you. There have been many times where I have been convicted with some truths that have been incredibly hard to sit with. But part of God's discipline is working out some of the areas of your heart that prevent you from being more like Him, that prevent you from being your best self. I believe this is why the Bible often gets misconstrued and mislabeled as hateful, because its truths are inconvenient to the lifestyles we live. Many people cherry-pick the parts of the Bible that make them feel good, rather than allowing conviction to do its work and hold them accountable for bringing their shortcomings to God for healing and restoration. The world sugarcoats sin, to make people feel more comfortable, or like they're not as bad as other sinners.

That's not the way God works. We all sin and fall short. In the eyes of our Lord, sin has no weight; Jesus came here to condemn sin and give us freedom through His death and resurrection. Jesus didn't come to earth to dance on flower petals and hug trees. He came here to permanently put His foot on the devil's neck and hug the sinners. He came here on a heavenly mission: to conquer the world so we could have eternal life through Him. God is all about His business when it comes to His precious children He loves so much.

The world is going to continue to mistake truth for hate. Nothing about the truth in the Bible is convenient, because we are living in a world full of sin and evil.

Do you want to know what is convenient?

The fact that our sins are paid for. The fact that we have a gift called grace that is absolutely free, and we don't have to work to earn it, and with that gift comes a lifestyle that encourages us to live, think, and act differently than the rest of the world. Through discipline, and through this lifestyle, we learn how to stop being offended when one of God's teachings or a word from the Bible comes to our attention and makes us uncomfortable or upset.

You might be able to relate. The reason you may feel offended or uncomfortable when faced with God's truths is because your soul is stirring, literally. Your soul is stirred when God wants to convict you of His truths. There is a deep, beautiful, intimate awakening that happens as you allow God to work in your heart to be more like His. The enemy works to ruffle the feathers of your heart, to make you feel that the stirring of your soul is an attack from God. I promise you, it's not. God will do whatever it takes to get your attention. And remember, the enemy wants you to feel offended.

Let me remind you once more that there are two forces constantly battling for control of your heart. The enemy loves to manipulate you and disguise God's conviction as offense. I am here to tell you to embrace the discomfort of conviction. God is doing something beautiful inside of you, but you must learn how to embrace it and press into what He is trying to teach you. When you get offended, you tend to use the offense as a reason to dismiss God. That is the enemy's tactic; it's exactly what he wants you to do. But when you press into God instead, He will reveal so much more. In that same process, you learn how to respond to offense with grace. You learn how to live and respond the same way Jesus did.

Remember, this is a building process, and God is patient.

God wants you to live outside your comfort zone. Because when we step out of our comfort zone and align ourselves more with His will, that is when God works through us. That is how God shines. That is how we lead others to Christ. Being confronted with God's truths is not to be mistaken for being attacked or hated. God is love. The Bible says Jesus was filled with grace and truth. That is how He wants us to live too.

Seeking God's will over our own will inevitably put us in times where we don't understand. That is exactly where God wants us.

> The fear of the Lord is the beginning of wisdom, and the knowledge of the Holy One is understanding. (Proverbs 9:10)

In order to be the best version of ourselves, we must allow God to discipline us, to teach us, and He does so when we take the time to study His Word intentionally. There are no spark notes or cheat sheets to heavenly understanding. The only way to better understand Him is to study His Word. Like I said, God rewards those who seek Him, and He rewards them with revelations and understanding into the heavenly treasures placed all throughout scripture. God teaches you how to make sense of the world that is dangerously walking in the opposite direction of Him; He will constantly remind you that you are on the right path and of the joy you have to look forward to in heaven.

Oh, brethren, be great believers! Little faith will bring your souls to heaven, but great faith will bring heaven to you.

—Charles Spurgeon

Many people see heaven as a destination. This is true, but the beauty of a relationship with Jesus is that heaven is both the present and the future. Your nearness to Him while you are here, on earth, gives us an idea of the wondrous and glorious future we have to look forward to once we get to heaven. A relationship with God is like a taste of heaven. It's filled with hope. It's filled with revelation. It's filled with joy. That is the recipe for getting to experience a life full of faith and purpose, while we wait to step into eternity with Him, in our real home. We can spend our time knowing that the best is still yet to come. It will be so worth the wait.

God Is the Teacher

Let me ask you a question:

In order to pass a test in school, you have to study first, right?

Studying is the only way to understand the material and get a good grade.

Believing in Jesus is passing the test. However, our discipline comes in spending the rest of our lives truly studying His Word, claiming His promises over our lives, and learning how to be more like Him. Not only must we seek His truths, but we must also pray for understanding.

God is the only One capable of proper guidance and discernment. He knows it is easy for us to get distracted, but the beauty of the nature of God is that He is with you, willing to teach you and be patient with you if you are willing to listen. That's why before God can do any work through you, He has to work in you. It's important for His Spirit to fill every ounce of you with His wisdom and understanding, because that is the only way to truly tune out the white noise of this world and tune in to the whispers of the Holy Spirit. That is the only way to learn how to handle the fragile hearts of others who do not know Jesus as the Savior of the world. God calls us to live differently, speak differently, walk differently, and shine differently than the rest of the world because that is how we are identified as soldiers of His Kingdom.

Denying yourself and taking up your cross means you are choosing not to live like the rest of the world. You don't have the same mission as them. You don't have the same mindset as them. You are a child of an Almighty King, who has an eternal destiny for you and desires to accomplish a heavenly purpose through you. But if I haven't already said it enough, it is absolutely critical that you accept and embrace the power of transformation that comes through discipline.

This transformation is the process of spiritual maturity. The whole point of a relationship with Jesus is that you continue to grow in wisdom and in truth, and apply those truths to the way you live your life. Spiritual maturity comes from not only hearing the Word but putting the Word into practice; in other words, obedience. As we become more obedient by practicing what the Bible and Holy Spirit instruct us to do, that is when we are becoming more and more like Him. As our character begins to transform into the likeness of His image, our discernment grows stronger. As our discernment grows stronger, we begin to obey His promptings and teachings more and more. We begin to think and act more like Him. This is because the more we know about what Jesus has done for the world, the more we want to live in a way that honors Him. In order to honor Him, we have to imitate what Jesus did and how He always responded to those who betrayed and even crucified Him.

The New Testament teachers had a lot to say about spiritual maturity, or rather the problem with immaturity. If you want to read about how Jesus Christ was the perfect fulfillment of the Old Testament, I encourage you to read the book of Hebrews. This book summarizes the power of faith, the power of His promises, and our guaranteed inheritance of those promises.

This is why the New Testament authors constantly encourage their brothers and sisters to keep the faith and pursue righteousness. There are many people (past, present, and future) who believe in Jesus and confess their belief in Christ, but they neglect to study His Word. They forget that part of planting the seed (the Word of God) is making sure we take the time to water the seed as well, so it can be firmly rooted in our hearts. If we don't, we risk the chance of distraction and falling away from His truths.

When I was in college, I was very good at anatomy. I also loved physiology and enjoyed learning about the bones, muscles, and organs of the human body. There are over six hundred muscles and approximately two hundred bones in the adult body. It's wild to think that God carefully knitted that many muscles and bones together. I would often carry around a stack of flashcards, so I could refresh my memory throughout the semesters of Anatomy I and Anatomy II. I knew anatomy so well that I would even get the bonus questions correct on my exams. I loved to study it. By the end of my second year of college, I could identify almost every single muscle and bone in the body.

The following semester, I switched majors. I didn't have to study anatomy and physiology anymore. It was knowledge I enjoyed acquiring, but I didn't need to apply it or practice it. My flashcards were put in a drawer. Since I no longer study these things, I can't remember them. It's hard to retain information, and it's easy to forget when you don't study it on a regular basis. If I were to pick up the subject of anatomy again, I would have to go back to the basics and start all over again.

If you don't continually feed your mind with the Word of God, you will not be able to retain His promises and instructions. It doesn't matter if you are a new believer or an experienced one. The Word is something you must continually feed your soul; it's the real soul food. Even after you accept the fact that Jesus passed the test for you, you must continue to study His Word and remain close to Him in order to harvest spiritual fruit in your life. The New Testament teachers tried to explain this to their fellow believers:

> We have a great deal to say about this, and it is difficult to explain, since you have become too lazy to understand. Although by this time you ought to be teachers, you need someone to teach you the basic principles of God's revelation again. You need milk, not solid food. Now everyone who lives on milk is inexperienced with the message about righteousness, because he is an infant. But solid food is for the mature—for those whose senses have been trained to distinguish between good and evil. (Hebrews 5:11–14)

The author further instructs us to leave behind the elementary teachings about Jesus, and press on to maturity. We are to completely immerse ourselves with the Word regularly, not just on Sundays. We are to meditate on it, pray over it, and soak our minds in truth. Doing this builds our knowledge and also our trust. The more you read His promises, the greater trust you have in His promises. As you build trust in His promises, you gradually learn how to lean on them and not your own understanding of things. God's promises have never failed. And they never will.

The transformation that comes with spiritual maturity is paired with the revelations of His heavenly truths. The more you learn, the more God reveals to you. In fact, be prepared to have your mind blown on a regular basis. Being a child of God is a privilege and a gift. It is to our benefit that we rest in the shadow of His protection. Don't ever let yourself forget the power you have as a child of God. You see, the enemy doesn't fear believers. The enemy fears the moment believers step into their true power that comes from allowing God to work in them, so He can manifest Himself in their hearts and allow Him to work through them. The enemy fears those who act in obedience, because for those who are submitted to God, they have a peace, a hope, and a faith that cannot be broken. The enemy knows that the Word of God gives us power and authority over his distractions and manipulative schemes; he is just hoping that *you* don't know that. God holds the trump card. Period.

Whatever you do, don't stop studying for the test, even though you've already passed it. I promise you, as you continue to study, you will never want to stop.

Building your knowledge of Him is what will enable you to walk confidently and boldly in His truths. People often defer to secondhand spirituality to learn about God. Devotionals and inspirational quotes are great, but there is nothing compared to immersing yourself in the written Word. I want to encourage you to do it old school. Get a hard copy of the Bible, grab a highlighter and a pen, and take notes. If you don't know a word or the city or nation it's referring to, look it up. In order to read and study the Bible, you need to be able to put it in context. Trust me, I've had to give myself some geography lessons as I put myself in the pages and write down those promptings I don't want to forget. Sit with it. Think about it. Pray over it. Ask God to help you understand. Journal while you're reading. Some of my biggest inspirations came from looking back at the notes I took when I was in a certain season of my life. This book is a product of those notes.

Reading scripture doesn't just allow you to gain understanding, but it builds your confidence. The notes you take, whether it is a mental note or a physical note, become the building blocks of faith. Your stillness, quiet time, and prayer with God allow you to recharge your biblical batteries.

Our strength comes from our continual dependence on Him.
Our peace comes from our continual focus on Him.
Our joy comes from our continual reassurance of His promises.
We need God to fill our cups, and He can only do that when we allow ourselves to rest in His Word. You can't pour from an empty

cup. The world demands your time, energy, and attention while you carry around the load needed in order to keep life in order. Jesus doesn't take; He gives. He fills. This is why rest must be a priority if we are going to embrace God's will and create a life that's more in alignment with His purpose for us. In fact, God believes in rest so much that on the seventh day, He Himself rested. Isn't it wonderful that we have a God Who tells us that the only way to build our strength is by resting in Him?

God created human beings, not human doings.

> Be still, and know that I am God. (Psalm 46:10 NIV)

Stillness allows God to make room in our hearts to show us His heavenly truths. The amount of wisdom and understanding that can be found within the text of the Bible is enough to keep our hearts and notebooks full of truth, until we are called to our heavenly home. The Bible is timeless, which means that it is always relevant in every season of our lives. It is not a book of the past; the Word of God is active and living today.

He is still just as powerful, faithful, and unchanging as He's always been.

CHAPTER 5
PAIN IN PERSPECTIVE

God wants us to experience a love for Him that goes so deep that He will use your pain to expose His magnificence and for His ultimate glory.

Think about it:

If God always spared us pain, we would never get to experience His miracles.

If God always spared us hardship, we would never get to experience his power.

If there were no such thing as death, we would never get to experience eternal life.

If you are like me, I'm sure you've spent countless hours of your life pleading to God, asking Him to take away the pain, the sickness, and the hurt. Suffering is not something we ask for, but it's a card we are inevitably dealt in the game of life. Physical and emotional battle wounds take a long time to heal. Some of us are still fighting for healing. It's a deep process.

Before Jesus handed Himself over to the Sanhedrin (the Jewish court) to be crucified, He went away to pray. Not only was Jesus about to give His life for the world, but He was about to be betrayed and denied by His very own disciples, Judas and Peter. His best friends were about to turn on Him. Jesus was already under enough pressure. He literally had the weight of the world on His shoulders. He knew what was about to happen. The Bible said Jesus was in so much anguish, that while He was praying, He began to sweat drops of blood. He even asked God to take the pain away: "Father, if you are willing, take this cup away from me—nevertheless, not my will, but yours, be done" (Luke 22:42).

"Not my will, but Yours."

Pain can sometimes disrupt our relationship with God, because we don't understand what His plans are. We don't understand what God is doing behind the scenes, even though deep down, we know God is good. Jesus knew what God's plan was. He knew the pain He was about to experience was going to accomplish God's ultimate purpose: to save the world. Jesus sets the perfect example for how we should be responding—with faith. He didn't want to experience the pain, but He was more concerned with God's will being done.

Jesus knows what real suffering is. It says in the Bible that during his life, he offered prayers of appeal, tears, and loud cries to the One Who was able to save Him from death. It says, "Although he was the Son, he learned obedience from what he suffered" (Hebrews 5:8).

If there is one thing adversity is designed to teach us, is that God does not respond to pain; He responds to faith. *Faith* is an action word. I'm not saying that God doesn't see your pain. Trust me, He does. However, He is more concerned with changing your heart rather than your circumstance. Faith, however, is built through questions; through prayer; by opening up and having a relationship with Him, so He is able to discipline your heart and teach you how to allow adversity to turn your faith into action rather than question. He teaches us what obedience looks like as He reminds us of His sovereignty. We must know Who is in control, because we sure aren't.

REST IN THE RAINBOW

God uses some of the darkest, most difficult times of our lives to break down the barriers of fear, anxiety, and doubt that surround our heart. We tend to put up a wall and push God away because in some messed-up way, we subconsciously believe that holding onto emotions of worry and fear gives us control of our situation. We live in a world that has an insatiable appetite for control, and we believe that contentment and happiness lie in our next level of achievement or relationship. We worry about our future, as if we can control the outcome.

Let me set this truth on your heart:

Whatever you are worried about, anxious about, or overwhelmed over, God has already got it all figured out. It's hard to trust what God is doing during uncertain times; I get it, but there's a reason the Bible tells us not to lean on our own understanding.

Understanding will never bring you peace. Faith truly begins when we stop trying so hard to understand. Faith is the greatest key to unlocking peace in our lives. God's way of thinking is much higher than ours. The Bible is the only way to decipher the meaning behind our struggles while illustrating the nature of God and the character of Jesus's heart, so you are able to find rest through believing in His promises, rather than the empty pursuit of happiness. Control and comparison will never lead to true contentment. The joy and grace we find in Jesus sustain us. Trusting God is the only way to displace fear and worry. Once we begin to confront our fears and our circumstances, and start viewing them as opportunities to build trust and dependence on Jesus and reminding ourselves that He is in control, God will go to work on our behalf.

See, faith isn't only an action word for us; it's an action word for God, as well. He requires your full dependence so He can show you He is in control. Relinquishing control is a scary thing, right? Society has conditioned us to think that life without control is a bad thing. Taking a leap of faith is kind of like jumping off a cliff into a body of water.

You. Just. Have. To. Take. That. Step.

The beautiful part about it, though, is that Jesus is always there to catch you. God knows that the more steps you take in faith, the more you are demonstrating to Him that you trust Him. That's how we build our trust in God, and it's how we grow in spiritual maturity, as well. You will be amazed what God reveals to you in the midst of your leaps of faith. The more you depend on God, the more He reveals to you. He has so much to teach us. His Spirit will whisper truths to your heart that will calm the winds of the stormiest seasons of our lives.

But remember, the key is faith. The key is in your hands. God goes before you, is always behind you, and always has His mighty hand within reach, but He cannot take that step for you.

Standing on God's promises is actually most applicable in situations we understand the least. Your perspective shifts when you spend more time with God, praying and reading His Word. Faith turns your focus to Him, so He can remind you, "Our momentary affliction is producing for us an absolutely incomparable eternal weight of glory" (2 Corinthians 4:17).

We have an eternity to look forward to in heaven. Scripture might just seem like words on a piece of paper to you, but when you take the time to let these words truly soak into your heart, they become more than just words. They take root. You can feel yourself growing and your perspective shifting, as you learn to claim those words you know are promises over your life. They become your lifeline, the only truth that makes sense. You start to understand what it means to have peace that surpasses human understanding. It is a joy and peace that this world is not capable of giving you.

God wants you to know that faith and trust bring great blessings and reward. This is something that is mentioned in the Bible thousands of times. Trusting God can be difficult at first. The power of what He can do in our lives is so great that it's hard to believe. Even when Jesus was alive, He performed so many miracles, and people still didn't believe He was the Son of God. It's hard for people to believe things they don't understand. But once you spend time with God and learn what He wants to do in your life, it becomes much easier to turn doubt into belief and count on the fact that He will turn your burdens into blessings, as long as you have the wholehearted faith to believe that He can.

Through the Fire

Life with Jesus is like a game of connect-the-dots.

It's important to understand that our pain has a very special purpose, and faith can only be refined through fire. How many times have you prayed to God, "Please, God. I know you can, I know you can, I know you can …"

Of course, He can; He's God.

But God is waiting for you to say, "God, I know you will."

That is the moment you have claimed a promise from Him.

> Dear friends, do not be surprised at the fiery ordeal that has come on you to test you, as if something strange were happening to you. But rejoice in it as much as you participate in the sufferings of Christ, so that you may be overjoyed when His glory is revealed. (1 Peter 4:12–13)

Faith is never supposed to be a last resort. It should always be our first instinct. It's time to shift our perspectives.

It's about looking at your earthly circumstances with a heavenly perspective. God wants to use us to display His glory to others. I'm going to give you an example of how claiming a promise completely changed my perspective and my relationship with God.

It was 2018, on New Year's Eve night. I went to a friend's house early in the evening but came home before the clock struck midnight because I couldn't hang. I decided I was going to ring in the New Year in bed, with my Yorkie pup and my Bible. I did not feel well that day. At all. In fact, I hadn't felt well all of 2018. My ulcerative colitis was the worst it had ever been. I had unintentionally lost thirty pounds in about three months. I had probably already had about thirty bloody bowel movements that day. That had been my new normal for a few months. Not only did I feel like a prisoner chained to the toilet, but I felt like a prisoner to my own body. My immune system had been in attack mode for the past two years, and my body was no longer able to keep up with the destruction going on inside.

My body was on fire, waging war against itself, and I physically felt like I was hanging by a thread. At that time, my body had stopped responding to treatment. My physical strength was gone, so my spiritual strength was the only thing I had left. At that time, I wasn't even sure what spiritual strength actually was, but I knew that the Word was the only thing I was holding on to.

I was reading the book of John that night. Side note: This is one of my most favorite books in the Bible. Reading the book of John is like putting your head right on Jesus's chest. You can feel the heartbeat of Jesus when you read that book. John loved Jesus so much, and reading it allows you to put yourself right in the middle of their relationship, as well as the miracles Jesus performed during His earthly ministry.

I was desperate for a miracle.

I came across John, chapter 9. That chapter is all about how Jesus healed a man who was born blind. The miracle was that Jesus restored the man's sight. He healed him. As Jesus and His disciples were walking past the man born blind, they asked Jesus, "Rabbi, who sinned, this man or his parents, that he was born blind?" In other words, they wanted to know what he did to deserve to be born without sight.

Jesus responded, "Neither this man nor his parents sinned. This came about so that God's works might be displayed in him" (John 9:3).

After Jesus said this, He spit on the ground to make mud, and spread it on the man's eyes. He instructed him to wash his eyes, and the man came back, with his sight restored.

The man went and professed to everyone that Jesus healed him.

It was truly a miracle. It is actually recorded in scripture that no one had ever heard of someone opening the eyes of a person born blind. Jesus knew what He was doing when He healed that man. He knew he would go and tell everyone what Jesus did for him. Jesus knew that man was going to give Him all of the glory.

So I made a promise to God that night; I guess you could call it my New Year's resolution. I decided to take a leap of faith that was going to force me to lose the control I thought I had over my chronic illness and medical situation. It was going to force me to check myself when the enemy's lies began to surface in my mind. It was going to force me to make my praise bigger than my problems. The leap of faith was choosing to surrender my worry, my pain, and my battle with chronic illness over to Him. It was time for me to truly let go, and let God work. I was going to claim John 9:3 over my life. I was going to claim victory and healing. I prayed and told God that after He healed me, I was going to tell the world Who did it. It was one of the hardest things I have ever done. It was time to put His teaching into practice. It was time for me to truly activate my obedience in Him.

A week later, I ended up in the emergency room. Another colonoscopy revealed that my prognosis was worse than I thought.

Three weeks later, I had my first reconstructive bowel surgery to remove my entire large intestine. I had been told my entire adult life that I could never be a candidate for bowel reconstruction. Experts in the field of gastroenterology told me it was impossible.

But I made a promise to God. As a matter of fact, I claimed His promise over my life. At this point, my life literally depended on it.

I've never fully surrendered a battle to God like I did on December 31, 2018. Now, I understand what happens when we put our full trust and wholehearted faith in God. Faith must always be accompanied with action. True faith requires a response from God, Who uses our darkest moments and deepest pain so He can go to work and show you the bigger picture He wants to paint over your life. But you have to trust Him in order for Him to show you that. Trusting is hard to do when you only rely on your own understanding, instead of a God Who has an impeccable track record for doing the impossible.

God's plan is so much bigger than we know. This book would not have been possible without the dark moments. God wants to use our pain to glorify Himself.

After all, He turned my impossible situation into a miracle of healing. The fifteen years of chronic illness and pain make sense now that I know, "this came about so that God's works might be displayed." He works in our lives to use our pain to showcase His glory. He wants to make sure we know when He turns impossible into possible, that it is all because of Him. He gets all of the glory.

That miracle was a product of fifteen years of prayer, and one act of pure faith and obedience. It's easy to convince yourself that God isn't listening to you. But I can tell you this: Sometimes, what really needs to happen is for you to listen to God. You may be in a similar place right now, waiting for God to answer a prayer, to give you a miracle. God doesn't always answer your prayers right away, because He wants to show you how to connect the dots between the pain and the promise. He needs you to listen to Him first. Always remember that God works in you, so He can work through you. Once you receive the promise, or God answers your prayers, you can look back and see all along how God was working the whole time.

That's why He says His power is perfected in our weaknesses (2 Corinthians 11:9). The areas of your life where you are the most hurt, experience the most pain, the most hardship, is exactly where God wants to work His biggest miracles. But we must lose our grip on trying to control our circumstances and allow God to show us exactly why He calls us conquerors, in Jesus's name. Our strength is truly not by our own, and it requires complete surrender of our battles in order for us to gain the right perspective. When you look at your earthly circumstances with an earthly perspective (without God), you will always feel the weight of the world on your shoulders. But when you look at your earthly circumstances through a heavenly lens, waves of peace and hope will build your confidence in Him and will sustain you, no matter how hard it seems, how difficult it appears, or how much hurt you may feel in the moment.

What I don't want to happen is for you to get through this chapter and think that God always answers prayers just because you "have faith." God is much deeper than that. We have to always remember that His ways of thinking are higher than our own. His will being done is far more beneficial for ourselves and others than what our will or plan might be.

The key to understand here is that God doesn't always answer our prayers in the way we hope or expect Him to, but I can assure you that through surrender, your perspective will shift; that is God's priority.

I promise you, if God had answered my prayers for healing on the first go-around, this book would not have been written. The pain would have taught me nothing, and it most definitely wouldn't have made me dependent on God. He had to do something in me, so He could do something through me. God put the moments of my pain in perspective, because He had an assignment for me after the test. Pain taught me discipline, and surrender taught me obedience. His promises are what shaped my perspective and helped me to better align myself with God's character and His will.

We should want nothing less than His will to be done in our lives.

If healing doesn't come on this side of the clouds, it is sure to come when we get to heaven. This is encouragement to allow God to show you how to connect the dots between our pain and His promises. After all, through Him, we have an eternity to look forward to. This life is only temporary.

As we use part 1 to help us understand how God works in us and in our hearts, we must fully understand this perspective first, in order to grasp how God wants to work through us. We are all called to look at life through a heavenly lens. This is not something that can be taught in school, only through a relationship with Jesus Christ.

He is with you, always. He is waiting for you to let go of control and grab hold of His hand.

CHAPTER 6
STEP INTO THE RING

Let me tell you something you already know. The world ain't all sunshine and rainbows. It's a very mean and nasty place, and I don't care how tough you are, it will beat you to your knees and keep you there permanently if you let it. You, me, or nobody is gonna hit as hard as life. But it ain't about how hard you hit. It's about how hard you can get hit and keep moving forward; how much you can take and keep moving forward. That's how winning is done! Now, if you know what you're worth, then go out and get what you're worth. But you gotta be willing to take the hits, and not pointing fingers saying you ain't where you wanna be because of him, or her, or anybody. Cowards do that and that ain't you. You're better than that! I'm always gonna love you, no matter what. No matter what happens. You're my son and my blood. You're the best thing in my life. But until you start believing in yourself, you ain't gonna have a life.

—Rocky Balboa

The World Ain't All Sunshine and Rainbows, But God's Promises Are

Rocky said it best: Nothing is gonna hit you as hard as life. Rocky Balboa is a classic example of what it takes to conquer fear and to be a champion. No matter how many times he was hit and knocked down in the ring, he continued to get back up. He stepped into the ring and refused to back down. He showed up. He took the hits. He got back up. Every. Single. Time.

If you've not watched any of the Rocky Balboa movies, you have my permission to place your bookmark right here and have a movie marathon.

Here's the thing: We are all human. We are designed to feel. We are allowed to have feelings, and we are allowed time to process them. We are allowed to be upset, and we are allowed to be disappointed. Sometimes, life can feel like waves of hit after hit after hit. Life's punches can hit so hard that you feel more suffocated than bruised. Disappointments are inevitable; they are part of the human experience.

However, dwelling in disappointment is what leads to discouragement. As a child of God, we are not supposed to be discouraged. We've all heard people say you can't control certain circumstances, but you can control how you respond to them. That's the key, right there. Understanding Who is in control starts with allowing what thoughts you choose to dwell on.

I feel like if it were Jesus speaking instead of Rocky, He would summarize that same statement like this:

You will have suffering in this world, but be courageous! I have conquered the world (John 16:33). So consider it pure joy, whenever you face trials of many kinds, because you know that the testing of your faith produces perseverance. Let perseverance finish its work so that you may be mature and complete, not lacking anything (James 1:2–4). After you have suffered for a little while, the God of all grace, who called you to His eternal glory in Me, will Himself perfect, confirm, strengthen, and establish you (1 Peter 5:10). You are blessed when they insult you and persecute you and falsely say every kind of evil against you because of Me. Be glad and rejoice, because your reward is great in heaven (Matthew 5:11–12). That is how winning is done! I am always going to love you, no matter what. In all these things you are more than conquerors through Him who loved you. Neither death nor life, nor angels nor rulers, nor things present nor things to come, nor powers, nor height nor depth, nor any other created thing will be able to separate us from the love of God that is in Christ Jesus your Lord (Romans 8:37–39). I am the way, the truth, and the life. No one comes to the Father except through Me (John 14:6).

Being in a relationship with God does not give you immunity from suffering or hardship. In fact, the Bible says it loud and clear that suffering is an intrinsic part of our human experience on earth. It's often common for believers in Jesus Christ to be persecuted, ostracized, or made fun of. Jesus was familiar with being hated. He took the hits, verbally and physically. He bore the weight and wrath of the world's sins on Himself. He knows what real pain is. He tells us not to be surprised when we experience suffering and a testing of our faith. However, this is meant to teach you to bring your suffering to Him to allow Him to teach you what you need to learn from it and how to better endure it. Life knocks you down on your knees to put you in the perfect posture to pray.

Prayer exercises our faith muscle. Without tension, muscles cannot get stronger: Bodybuilding 101. Our struggles and hardships will always be disappointing, but you know that with God, you are never a victim of your circumstances. Our victory is always eternal citizenship in heaven. Death is actually when we cross the victory line.

Faith is what enables us to show up every day, no matter how many times we get knocked down. His mercies are new every single day, and that alone is a good enough reason to get back up, step into the ring, and fight another round. Faith, as long as it's activated, is our guaranteed strength.

I've said it once, and I'll say it again: We have to remember that pain is necessary for God to accomplish His purpose in us. However, you will never be able to stand the testing of your faith or pursue your purpose if you allow fear to be stronger than faith. Bravery requires vulnerability, and most times, God requires brokenness in order for you to discover how He wants to use you to advance His kingdom and your heavenly mission. Perseverance and strength are the only results to come out of stepping into something that has the potential to knock you to your knees. Faith is your strongest weapon against adversity.

That's how winning is done.

Every time you turn your focus on God instead of your problems, He will polish your faith a little bit more, and you will come out a little bit stronger, with a little more fight. Every time you take captive the familiar thoughts that creep up in your mind that are not from God, and replace them with His truths, His promises, and His reminders of His love for you, you will come out a little bit stronger and with more wisdom and discernment of God's guiding, loving, and convicting voice. It works every single time. He never promises it's going to be easy, but He does promise you strength to endure hardships. Our faith will never have a destination until we reach heaven, of course. Our faith will never be perfect. It's a good thing we're not required to be.

It's okay to feel weak, as long as we bring our insecurities to God and let Him heal our hearts and fix the areas where we lack confidence. It's okay to shake your fist at God. Tell God your frustrations, but don't turn your back on Him. Sometimes, in order to build your faith, you will wrestle with God. He isn't surprised by your doubts. He knows that faith is built through questions. Your questions will never shock or offend Him. God is completely capable of handling your vent sessions and your questions. We see in the Bible where God gives reassurance to His children over and over again, telling them to be strong, to be courageous, and to not be afraid. In so many places in the Bible, we see what happens when people divert to their own strength to carry them through and use their own understanding. We also see what happens when people rely on God's strength, on His promises, and not their own understanding. The results are two totally different outcomes.

Equipped for Battle

Strength doesn't always have to come in the form of a big, fiery flame when you know who your Protector is. In fact, the Bible never tells us to rely on our own strength in any situation.

> Finally, be strengthened by the Lord by his vast strength. Put on the full armor of God so that you can stand against the schemes of the devil. (Ephesians 6:10)

Paul instructs us to strengthen ourselves in the Lord. We develop this strength and express it by intentionally covering ourselves in the full armor of God. Notice that Paul didn't say, "Grab your guns and grenades, and get ready for a bloodbath." He introduces the idea of the full, symbolic armor of God that every believer needs in order to stand against the enemy and his attacks. At this point, we know what the schemes of the enemy are. The enemy wants nothing more than to divide, distract, and deter us from being close to God. As believers in Christ, we have a permanent bullseye on our backs. As long as we are breathing and standing in truth, grace, faith, unity, courage, and everything else the good news of the Gospel represents, we are going to be attacked. The better equipped you are, the more you are able to recognize the battle for what it is.

When Paul talked about spiritual warfare in his letter to the churches in Ephesus, he was talking about a battle between good and evil. Paul wrote the book of Ephesians while in the custody of Roman soldiers, yet he encouraged the churches to understand that our Christian struggle is not against flesh and blood, but against the darkness of evil and the spiritual forces of heaven. You better believe that when you are walking in God's will and purpose, the enemy will hit you with all he's got. That is why it's important to be suited and strapped in the Word of God.

> Stand, therefore, with truth like a belt around your waist, righteousness like armor on your chest, and your feet sandaled with readiness for the gospel of peace. In every situation take up the shield of faith with which you can extinguish all the flaming arrows of the evil one. Take the helmet of salvation and the sword of the Spirit—which is the word of God. (Ephesians 6:14–17)

This type of spiritual strength, paired with the full armor of God, can only truly go to work when we have made time to understand how to put on every piece of this armor—through prayer and time spent with God and in His Word.

If you want to wear truth like a belt, you must study truth.

If you want to wear righteousness like a piece of armor on your chest, you must understand that righteousness is not earned; it is received through faith in Jesus.

If you want to strap your feet with the Gospel of peace, then you need to know what the Gospel says about unity.

If you want to properly use your shield of faith, then you must be perceptive to the persistent attempts the enemy will make to put a wedge between you and God, to weaken your faith.

If you want to put on the helmet of salvation, you must know the source of our heavenly hope.

And if you want to effectively fight with the sword of the Spirit, you must know scripture.

We are in a spiritual war, and we must make sure we have the right equipment for battle, so when the enemy looks at a child of God, he sees a warrior, covered in God's protection and victorious by His strength. The victory is always ours, because it is already His. The enemy doesn't want you to know the power and strength you have as a child of God. It thwarts his plans and exposes his weakness. Stinks for him.

The most admirable form of strength is in people who know the source of their strength. It has nothing to do with your power and everything to do with the promises that are evidence of our secured victory. Strength is about trusting and believing in the promise, and not the way we think or expect the promise to work out. If we know and trust that God works everything out for our ultimate good, then we can trust what He is doing, even if we don't understand.

Notice that every piece of the armor of God talked about by Paul is made for our defense. The only weapon we have for our offense is the sword, which is the Word of God. The sword is the only battle weapon we have, while the rest of the armor of God is made for us to defend ourselves with. There is a reason we must put on the full armor of God every day, which is our protection from the enemy. Trust me when I say that the enemy doesn't sleep. He throws darts and arrows 24/7. The armor is our protection. Without it, we are vulnerable to the enemy's attacks. We have the Word of God as our sword to remind the enemy who he's messing with.

This world is a battlefield, so step into the ring, and be prepared to take the hits. You are protected. The world needs spiritual warriors who know how to fight with the right type of spiritual gear. Believe in the power of His promises. Believe what He says about you. And always show up for the next round.

God will always meet you there.

CHAPTER 7
FUNCTIONAL FAITH

A child can teach us a lot about faith. The most authentic form of faith can be found within the convictions of a child. Several years ago, a coworker and I were helping out with fluoride cleanings for a preschool class. Next in line for a cleaning was a small, sweet girl who came confidently up to the table. We greeted one another with a big smile.

I asked the little girl, "How are you doing?"

Without hesitation, she responded, "Goooood. I was sick, but I asked Jesus to heal me, and He did."

The conviction that came out of that four-year-old's mouth was a declaration of confidence in Jesus. It was a testimony I'll never forget. She gave the purest example of how faith works. She asked, she believed, and she received. You see, God made it so easily accessible for us to receive Christ, that even a child can believe and have faith.

Faith is more than just believing God can; it's believing that God is faithful to fulfill His promises to us. We live in a world where people use the word *faith* very casually and without intention. Actually, faith is the boldest decision we could ever make. Functional faith is activated faith. It's audacious; it's courageous; it's adventurous. When you decide to walk by faith and not by sight, it's like walking confidently in the dark and trusting God that you won't hit a brick wall. We can't see God, but we can activate our faith by listening for that quiet, soft voice that is instilled in every single one of us.

That quiet voice soon becomes a familiar voice, a voice we know and trust. Relying on God is more than just dramatic leaps of faith; it's about the baby steps we take on a daily basis. When you fully and wholeheartedly rely on unwavering faith and trust in God, you must understand that your direction, guidance, and peace come from things you cannot see or fully understand. Faith and logic are polar opposites. This is why the Bible instructs us not to rely on our own understanding, because if we do, we will stumble over worldly confusion and frustrations. Through dependence on Him, faith transforms our minds and places a new perspective in our heart.

Many times, we ask God for things and hope He will provide, rather than believing He will. The reason for this is because we are so used to the world disappointing us. We fail to be bold in our faith because we've been disappointed too many times. We also fail to realize that the only reason God answers our prayers with a no is because His ways and His plan for our lives are much higher and better than we can imagine ourselves. Sometimes, when people ask God for something, he doesn't answer their prayers. We tend to think that God isn't listening or doesn't hear us. But faith is more than just prayers. It's about the willingness and audacity to lean into the journey of our walk with Jesus; it's a trust-building process. Faith is so much more than just a Sunday ritual. Faith is about learning how to live in complete dependence on Him daily, with a heart and ears keen to His voice. It's about trusting Him to direct our steps and leaving the outcomes up to Him. All of them.

Faith requires you to be in for it all or nothing at all. This is the most difficult part about faith to practice and apply in our lives. We want to give our worries and our problems to God, and we try to trust, but we still worry about our problems like they still belong to us. Activating faith means allowing God to discipline your heart, so your thoughts will shift to a higher way of thinking as you lean on Him and not your own understanding. Faith and discipline work together in everything you do, encouraging you in every step.

Faith Is an Act of Obedience

Faith is our heavenly hope, but while we are here on earth, it is so much more than that. Faith is what must be the foundation of our lives, so we can take confident steps in obedience and surrender to the One we place our hope in. Faith isn't just a belief; it's an action word that requires effort.

> In the same way, faith by itself, if it is not accompanied by action, is dead. (James 2:17)

There are some very practical implications when it comes to faith. Faith is not some fluffy, feel-good word we use. We tend to treat faith mildly and with heartless conviction. We can tell others to "just have faith," but we too often tend to gloss over the power of faith when we forget to remind ourselves of the promises of God. We must do better. Faith is about hope in the hard, but it's more than just believing God is good and He will get you through it. True, genuine faith is about learning how to endure and embrace trials; it's about learning how to control your tongue; it's about understanding how to separate worldly discernment from the wisdom and knowledge of the Word of God; it's about allowing the convictions of your heart and the Holy Spirit to discipline you as you learn the character of Jesus.

Just like surrender begins the building process in your life, faith operates the same way. Faith is not something you magically find; it's something you build intentionally and persistently. Understanding this will help you understand why pain and adversity are absolutely necessary to build your faith. In order to get through the valleys and reach your mountaintops, your legs must become stronger in order to climb. Faith is what allows you to reach the mountaintop and overcome adversity, but it shows us just how beautiful your journey is and how you can be more rooted in your faith during the next stormy season of your life. The deeper your faith grows, the more you will need to depend on God. That is exactly where He wants you to be. God knows that the stronger your faith grows, the less tempted you are to deal with your trials with fear, worry, and anxiety. Obedience to Him and trusting His promises is faith in action.

Faith Is Our Salvation

We are declared righteous through faith. When the day comes that we are face to face with Jesus, we will be judged by our works (I know what you may be thinking, but keep reading). We will get to the throne of heaven, where we either inherit the promise of eternity with Jesus, or are sent to a different type of eternity, in hell, where there will be weeping and gnashing of teeth, where people will be tormented in an immortal body that will be set on fire, forever. The Bible calls it the lake of fire. There will be a judgment day when our eternity is determined and finalized. However, we are saved through faith: When those who believe with their hearts and confess with their mouth that Jesus is their Savior, He intercedes for us in His heavenly courtroom.

> Therefore, he is able to save completely those who come to God through him, since he always lives to intercede for them. (Hebrews 7:25)

When we face judgment, those who are saved will, in fact, not be judged by their works. We will approach the throne to be judged, and Jesus will intercede by saying, "I know this one. This one is mine." You will be placed at the right hand of the throne of God, and the King will say to you:

> "Come, you who are blessed by my Father; inherit the kingdom prepared for you from the foundation of the world" (Matthew 25:34).

Your faith is what allows you to inherit the promise of heaven. Recall the worth-based mentality that was discussed in chapter 1. For those who come to the throne who do not know Jesus, they will indeed be judged by their works. They will finally see that their self-righteousness was never enough, their good deeds were never enough, and they will pay the cost for not accepting Jesus's free gift of salvation. Those who are judged will be placed on the left side of the throne of God to be sent to the lake of fire, where He will say:

> "I never knew you. Depart from me, you lawbreakers!" (Matthew 7:23)

We must remind ourselves that Jesus came to give us a new promise. Jesus is the mediator and the intercessor for us, so those who are called can receive the promise of an eternal inheritance. The old covenant ministry, a.k.a. a person's righteousness before God, was based on adherence to the law and with sacrificial offerings. The new covenant ministry is based on the body of Jesus, a.k.a. the Spirit of God Himself, as a sacrificial offering to bear the sins of the world. Because of the blood of Jesus, God's grace is enough to redeem us and make us righteous through Him, by His grace. And because of this new promise, the old promise is now null and void. We are inaugurated to a brand-new way of living. We no longer have to make offerings for sin.

> For by one offering he has perfected forever those who are sanctified. (Hebrews 10:14)

Instead, we choose to accept Him into our lives, so we can learn how to trust and act with the flavor of what grace has done for us. We are called to live by faith. We are called to love others with the same grace that covers us. If you want to get an even deeper perspective on how faith operates, I encourage you to read the book of Hebrews and the book of James in the New Testament.

The simplest definition of faith goes like this:

> Now faith is the reality of what is hoped for; the proof of what is not seen. (Hebrews 11:1)

We can't see Jesus, but we believe in Him. No matter how berserk or harsh this world gets, if you've placed your faith in Jesus, you are on the winning side. Welcome to Team Jesus.

Faith is a declaration of victory. Christ's victory on the cross was the catalyst to our faith. He has overcome the world. We win.

Our hope does not rest in what's to come during our earthly time here. Our hope rests in eternity with Him. We can have rest now, and we can have peace now. No matter what happens in life, when we get to be with Him in heaven, whenever that day comes, we are going to be so unbelievably blown out of our minds, in jaw-dropping awe of the wonders of heaven and at our Creator.

Will we be able to speak? When we are surrounded by His glory and in His presence, will we be dancing for joy, or will we even be able to stand? What will we see?

My hope lies in the fact that one day, we will find out. We will finally understand what Paul meant when he said our momentary suffering is small, compared to the glory that is going to be revealed to us. He was talking about heaven. The mission is heaven. It's always been about heaven. The true essence of the phrase, "the best is yet to come," is alluding to heaven.

Chapter 11 of the book of Hebrews recounts the power of faith and all the ways people in the Bible allowed faith to dictate their walk with God and the direction of their life. The author of

Hebrews explained that the prophets "by faith conquered kingdoms, administered justice, obtained promises, shut the mouths of lions, quenched the raging of fire, escaped the edge of the sword, gained strength in weakness, became mighty in battle, and put foreign armies to flight" (Hebrews 11:33–34). The author goes into detail about examples of people who lived by faith.

If faith holds the power of salvation, don't you think faith holds the power of God to fulfill a heavenly calling through you as well?

Faith Is Rewarded

The ultimate reward is heaven. The bigger your faith is, the bigger your blessings will be. You are allowed to believe for amazing, beautiful, powerful things to happen in your life. But God must be included in your plans. As a matter of fact, He must be the one responsible for directing your steps (Proverbs 16:9). Anything in life that is accomplished outside God's will must turn to ashes. Many of us have faced disappointment when something falls apart that we worked incredibly hard for. Faith allows you to accept that God's plan is the best plan, even if it doesn't make sense at the time, or we don't understand it. Even when our plans and relationships fail, God is still working.

You must keep working, too. Even through disappointments, you must keep pursuing Him.

Faith is a choice that changes everything. There are so many blessings out there with your name on them; they're just waiting for you to believe in them first. What God can accomplish in you is proportional to how much you depend on Him. Choose faith always, and see what happens. I promise that you have nothing to lose and everything to gain.

We should never get tired of honoring God and doing the right thing. We have a God Who holds the entire world in the palm of His hands; do not think that the things you do out of love for Him ever go unnoticed. God does not keep track of your transgressions, but He does remember everything you do out of your love for Him and for His Kingdom.

The type of faith God desires to reward is an audacious faith. If we know and believe that nothing is impossible for God, then why don't we start acting like it?

God is searching and working in the hearts of His children to bring up warriors who dare to pray bold and audacious prayers. Even Jesus said to His disciples, "Truly I tell you, if you have faith the size of a mustard seed, you will tell this mountain, 'Move from here to there,' and it will move. Nothing will be impossible for you" (Matthew 17:20).

If God can do a lot with a little faith, can you imagine what He will do with a big faith?

There's only one way to find out. There is a blessing out there with your name on it. I dare you to believe bigger.

CHAPTER 8
DROP YOUR ANCHOR

Let's talk about hope.

Hope is a by-product of grace. We hope for an eternity in heaven, because of what Jesus did on the cross. Without this sacrifice, there would be no way to get to heaven; humanity would be doomed, to be quite honest with you. So when we talk about hope, we are ultimately talking about hope that is not of this world, but of a Kingdom to come.

Hope is what builds the bridge between earth and heaven, and when the Bible talks about hope, you can see that it refers to a living hope, which is securely fastened to heaven. True hope is in an eternity to look forward to with Jesus.

The apostle Peter can tell us this, as a firsthand witness to the life and death of Jesus. Many of us live as if this world will be the end of life, but what Peter reminds people of, is that this world is not our home; we have an eternal citizenship in heaven. Even the end of this world is the beginning of heaven.

Although God wants us to enjoy life, He also wants us to rest in the promise of eternity with Him. In fact, that is where true joy comes from. It doesn't matter how bad life gets; we can always hope in the one thing that will not disappoint us:

> Therefore, with your minds ready for action, be sober-minded and set your hope completely on the grace to be brought to you at the revelation of Jesus Christ. (1 Peter 1:13)

Peter didn't stop there; he was on fire with the Word of God:

> You are being guarded by God's power through faith for a salvation that is ready to be revealed in the last time. You rejoice in this, even though now for a short time, if necessary, you suffer grief in various trials so that the proven character of your faith—more valuable than gold which, though perishable, is refined by fire—may result in praise, glory, and honor at the revelation of Jesus Christ. (1 Peter 1:5–7)

If we don't accept the fact that earthly suffering is inevitable and necessary, we will never be able to fully embrace the impact God wants to have in our lives. In fact, a common theme in all the books of the Bible is that they were all written during times of pain and suffering. Another common theme is that throughout the pain and suffering, the leaders and prophets clung to hope. While we hope in the promises of God to deliver us from earthly trials, we also hope in a heaven that will be revealed to us one day. As we focus and meditate on the true definition of hope, we slowly but surely begin to understand how grace sustains us and hope encourages us in what we have to look forward to.

It has historically been common for many believers to adopt anchors as a symbol of hope. Much of that reasoning comes from our author in the book of Hebrews, who says, "We have this hope as an anchor for the soul, firm and secure" (Hebrews 6:19).

In reality, every boat needs an anchor to prevent it from drifting. Fisherman will use an anchor, which is attached to a chain, to maintain their position in their favorite fishing spot. Others will use it to wade closer to shore and prevent their boat from drifting into the shore or into another boat.

When used properly, anchors serve only one purpose in nature: to hold a boat secure and steady. Once the anchor is dropped and hits the bottom, the boat cannot be budged. The waves cannot push the boat farther than what the anchor will allow. The anchor keeps the boat on a tight leash.

The anchor was birthed as a key symbol during the third century, when Christians were heavily persecuted under the Roman Empire. They were persecuted to such a degree that their lives were threatened for practicing their faith; they were not allowed to use or wear their cross in public, since that represented a symbol of their faith in Jesus Christ. This was also during a time when Christianity was a new (and dangerous) faith movement among those who believed. To be clear, the persecution of Christians has happened since Jesus walked the earth. Our Savior Himself was persecuted at the hands of religious Pharisees, chief priests, and the government. Christians are still persecuted to this day.

It's important to highlight the fact that the cross represents two entirely different things, depending on which era you are referring to, as well as the beautiful connection between the two. The reason Jesus hung on a cross was because during that time, the cross was a death sentence for criminals. The cross was a form of execution and a symbol of shame for the worst-of-the-worst Jewish criminals. The cross, before Jesus, was a dreadful symbol. However, Jesus turned horror into hope the moment He rose from the dead. Now, because of what Jesus did, the cross represents hope in the fact that there is life after death. Jesus turned the symbol of death into the symbol of eternal life. He picked a time in history in which death was sentenced in the most torturous way and turned it into the most beautiful spectacle of love.

> He erased the certificate of debt, with its obligations, that was against us and opposed to us, and has taken it away by nailing it to the cross. (Colossians 2:14)

Hope represents a perfect sacrifice that washed our sins clean with His own blood. Hope represents the God Who loved the world so much that He gave His only Son. Hope represents eternity for those who believe in Him. Hope represents a Holy Spirit Who lives in every single one of us, because of what happened on the cross. Hope is finding rest in His promises, because His promises anchor our souls.

Crux Dissimulata

During this time of Christian persecution, the anchor was regarded as a symbol of hope, but not because of the fact that it was an actual anchor. Since Christians were not allowed to bear their cross in public, they got skillfully creative with it. In other words, they dressed up the cross to disguise it as something else, so people were not able to associate it with the actual life-saving, life-giving cross. They disguised their faith with a particular symbol so they could recognize one another and secretly share their faith. Early Christians adopted the *crux dissimulata*. *Crux* is Latin for "cross," and *dissimulata* is a Latin word meaning "pretending or dissimilar." Here is an example of what it looks like; this symbol has also been found in ancient catacombs:

In this image, it is evident to see a similar version of the cross, which is resting on the foundation of two ichthus, or fish, which is a pagan symbol that represents Christianity as well. We had some very smart and creative ancestors. It is also easy to see how this ancient symbol looks very similar to an anchor; it was adopted as a branding icon to indicate the truth behind hope and show how the Bible is metaphorically and literally the anchor for our soul.

Many of us are blessed to live in places where we are able to freely and openly practice and share our faith, but the anchor still remains a symbol for those who put their trust and hope in Jesus. Hope is real, Jesus is real, and our Bible is the tangible evidence of this. We can trust it as if our life depends on it—because, quite frankly, it does.

Hope is our chain to heaven, and the anchor is His promises. But here's the thing: We must learn to be intentional about anchoring those promises to our heart. Imagine it like this: In this life, we all have a boat to live in. In fact, we're all just riding the waves of life. We aim to live our lives in a way that is always sailing in the right direction. Sometimes, we get lost at sea. We get back on track, and we get lost again. We go through periods of life in calm waters, soaking in the sun, and then we go through periods of rough waters and stormy seasons, where we feel like the sun is nowhere to be found. Sometimes, the waves feel like the ups and downs of a rollercoaster ride. I don't know about you, but sometimes I feel that the waters are totally polluted and darkened with worldly corruption. That's another topic for another day (or another book).

A Boat That Won't Budge

There are two types of people in this world: those who keep the anchor in the boat with them, and those who drop their anchor and let it hit the bottom.

We all have access to the same anchor, which is the Word, and the hope we have in Jesus, Who secured that for us when He died on the cross. But some of us have not learned how to use our anchor properly; in other words, we have not learned how to rest in God's promises. Even a good fisherman knows that an anchor that stays in the boat serves no purpose, and when the waves come, the boat will be pushed and tossed around. But for those who drop their anchor, although they might not be able to see the anchor, they can hope that the anchor is chained and will always hold. Their boat will not budge.

God's promises work the same way. In order for you to fully experience His promises, you have to drop your anchor. We must use His promises against the waves of adversity. It's easy to rest in God's promises when the waters are calm and the sun is shining, when everything in our life seems to be going well. A lot of times, we see the storm clouds rolling in and want to pull up our anchor and hurry to shore, or the stormy seasons of our life catch us completely off guard, and we forgot to drop our anchor in the first place. Essentially, we forget what God says. Just so you know, He has something to say about every season and every rain cloud in our life.

Let us always remember what God says when our boats begin to rock. And in case you've ever had a hard time trusting God, you're not alone. Jesus's disciples had a first-hand experience with needing a reminder of this, too.

You can see this story recounted throughout the Gospels of Matthew, Mark, Luke, and John. One day, shortly after Jesus miraculously fed five thousand people from five loaves of bread and two fish (no biggie, right?), He sent His disciples to wait for Him in a boat, while He went up to a mountain to pray. I'm sure after that miracle, Jesus needed time to give God thanks and praise. It says in Matthew that meanwhile, the boat had drifted pretty far from the land, and the boat was battered from the intensity of the waves, because the wind was against them (Matthew 14:24). By this time, it was morning, when the disciples saw Jesus approaching the boat, walking on water. They were immediately afraid, because they thought it was a ghost. I have to say I'd be a little nervous, too. Jesus spoke to them and said, "Have courage! It is I. Don't be afraid." Peter was still a little hesitant, so He told Jesus that if it was really Him, to command him to step outside the boat and walk to Him.

Jesus said, "Come."

Peter, with his eyes fixated on Jesus, got out of the boat and began to walk on water as well.

> But when he saw the strength of the wind, he was afraid, and beginning to sink he cried out, "Lord, save me!" (Matthew 14:30)

All it took was for Peter to take his eyes off Jesus for a split-second, and the storm had become his focus. He focused on his fears more than his faith in Jesus. But guess what happened next?

The Bible says that Jesus immediately reached out His hand and saved Peter, put him back in the boat, and rebuked the wind and stilled the waters. If the wind and waves obey God, then we can trust that He has complete control over the storms of our lives.

I'm not telling you to go out to sea and try to walk on water. What I am saying, though, is that when you keep your mind and your heart fixed on Jesus, you will be more focused on His promises than your problems. But the moment you lose focus on Him and overwhelm yourself with the wind and the waves of the storm going on around you, you are more tempted to listen to the voice of fear, doubt, and worry, which always accompanies waves of adversity.

Remember, adversity trains us to trust Him. Our anchor is in Him. This doesn't mean the waves won't batter our boats, but it does mean that no matter how hard the waves hit, our boat won't budge. We are secure in His promises. He is our stronghold. God wants to teach us how to trust Him, because He knows that living in dependence on Him is crucial to truly shaping our identity, revising our perspective on life, and making sense of the world around us. Trials in our life are just target practice for keeping our focus on Him. The more you keep your focus on Him, the more you will find rest in His promises, and the deeper understanding you will have about the nature of God and the character of Jesus.

The beautiful part about Jesus, though, is that even when you feel yourself drowning, like the waves of life are suffocating you, just look up and call on His name. He is always there to rescue you, stretching out his powerful, nail-scarred hand.

After all, we have a Savior Who walks on water.

CHAPTER 9
REMEMBER YOUR STONES

Take a moment to look back on all the things you have overcome in life.

I don't know about you, but I can't recall one time where God has ever failed me. In those hard, dark moments, it was hard for me to understand what He was doing. Why things happened the way they did didn't make sense back then. Even during the seasons of my life when I didn't have a relationship with God, I can see now that He was moving, even when the things I went through were a direct result of my own sin and disobedience. When I really take the time to think about it, the prayers that went unanswered, or the prayers that God responded to with a big, heavenly "NO," are the prayers I am thankful didn't play out the way I had hoped.

I know I am in good company when I say I am thankful for unanswered prayers.

Nothing in this world happens by coincidence. Every moment of our lives is divinely orchestrated by our heavenly Father, Who has counted the hairs on our heads and already knows the amount of breaths we will take in our lifetime. God knows us better than we know ourselves, and He has always been fully committed to meeting our needs.

There are some questions we have for God, though, that we might not ever know the answers to. There are some things that happen to us, and others, that we do not understand. I still have a lot of questions for God that I want Him to answer when I get to heaven. But through discipline and faith, we can believe and accept that God's ways of thinking are much higher than ours, and so are His plans. Our God is a good God, Who loves His children very much. We know this because of what Jesus did. Sometimes, I wonder what it must have felt like for God to pour out His wrath on His one and only Son that day on the cross. The One person who didn't deserve it is the One Who endured it all. It wasn't fair, but it served a very necessary purpose, and without it, there would be no salvation.

Although it seems melancholy, we mark our calendars to celebrate the death of Jesus, because we know what happened on Day Three. We celebrate the stone that was removed from the tomb Jesus was buried in, which indicated His resurrection from the dead. We take time to remember what those days were about, because while it may not have made sense at the time, we can see now that God was faithful in fulfilling His promise. He was faithful in redeeming humanity, which was His plan all along.

Chapter 3 in the book of Joshua starts off as a dialogue between God and the prophet. Actually, I wouldn't quite call it a dialog; God was speaking, and Joshua was listening and obeying His instructions. After Moses passed away, Joshua, the new leader in Israel, had been tasked by God to lead his people to a new land. Long story short, this was not an easy assignment, but Joshua continuously sought God's guidance, and he accepted His instructions and acted upon them. Joshua was very familiar with the miracles God did in Moses's life. The Lord was instructing Joshua to cross the Jordan River, just as Moses crossed the Red Sea on dry land forty years prior.

God told Joshua, "Today I will begin to exalt you in the sight of all Israel, so they will know that I will be with you just as I was with Moses. Command the priests carrying the ark of the covenant: When you reach the edge of the water, stand in the Jordan" (Joshua 3:7–8). God was brewing another miracle. That's what God does, ya know. And Joshua had a track record of believing and trusting in what God said, so he did exactly what he was told.

It's important to know that in Old Testament times, the Ark of the Covenant symbolized God's presence. If you look for yourself, you can see how God used the symbol of the ark to provide safety to the Israelites. This ark was an ornate wooden chest that Moses had built, that contained the tablet of the Ten Commandments and was something that Levitical priests carried with them among the Israelites. Check out the book of Exodus; Moses explains it best.

As Joshua, the priests, and the people of Israel walked to the Jordan River, this is what God did next:

> But as soon as the priests carrying the ark reached the Jordan, their feet touched the water at its edge and the water flowing downstream stood still, rising up in a mass that extended as far as Adam, a city next to Zarethan. The water flowing downstream into the Sea of Arabah—the Dead Sea—was completely cut off, and the people crossed opposite Jericho. (Joshua 3:15–16)

Thousands of people crossed the Jordan River that day. This was all in the middle of flood season, I might add.

God proved to Joshua, as well as the entire nation of Israel, that when you follow the Lord, heed His instruction, and trust in His promise, He will not only go before you and protect you, but He will defy the laws of nature to prove to His people that He. Is. God. Nothing is impossible for Him. God had an important lesson for the nation of Israel to learn from this miracle, and He wanted to make sure they remembered this story, too. So while everyone was crossing, God had Joshua summon a man from each of the twelve tribes of the people, to take twelve stones from the middle of the Jordan and bring them to where they spent the night, which ended up being the city of Gilgal.

Once they set up camp, Joshua told his people that the twelve stones they brought with them will forever be a memorial to the Israelites of what God did for them on that day. So when future generations asked them the meaning behind the stones, they would remember the promise God gave them, the miracle of what happened in the Jordan River, and others would know the mighty power of God's hand (Joshua 4:23–24). It's important to point out that it was not Joshua's idea to set up the memorial stones; it was God's. God's glory and power is too good to keep to ourselves, and He intended for the fulfillment of His promises and His mighty miracle to be a testimony to future generations, to teach others about Him.

What are your stones?

When I look back in time, I can think of so many times God has brought me out of the pit. I can recall the miracles I've witnessed because of Him. I remember the times I reached for God's hand, and He was always right there. I have many metaphorical stones that remind me that God has been with me, as well as with others. I've heard others share their stories of how God has been with them, delivered them from suffering, and worked miracles in their lives. The reason God wanted Joshua to use memorial stones was so they could share the story with others, future generations.

Your stones are your story. There is evidence of God in your testimony. The point of finding God is that when you do, you are compelled and moved to tell people how you found Him. You tell others about what He has done for you and how He has fulfilled His promises to you. That's how people learn about God, as well as what Jesus Christ came here to do. My friends, that is why the Bible was written—so that others could learn about the almightiness of God's miracles and the stories of those who were transformed by Jesus.

Your story is meant to serve the same purpose. We are put on this earth not only to love, honor, and glorify God, but to allow our love for God to manifest within us in a way that pours onto others, so the Holy Spirit can be seen in us and witnessed by others. That is how we allow God to begin His work through us.

But it doesn't stop there.

Once you remember all the ways God has showed up for you, you begin to show up for yourself differently. The real transformation occurs when you are more aware that your strength, your identity, and your struggle are shaping you into a powerful form of God's testimony. We may not have the Ark of the Covenant to carry with us these days, like the Levitical priests, but we have our Bible, full of His promises and miraculous testimonies.

Remember your stones; make your heart a memorial for all God has done for you, because His work in you is not finished yet. Allow God to discipline you, shine through your life, influence others, and be your constant reminder that "I will be with you, just as I was with Moses. I will not leave you or abandon you" (Joshua 1:5).

God is in the business of transformation, not stagnation. A lot of times, though, we tend to get stuck in the transition of God doing something in our lives because the moment we get uncomfortable, we fight back. The moment the enemy whispers lies, we begin to doubt ourselves, doubt God. The losses we have in life are not to be downplayed or taken lightly, but as you allow yourself to lean into the character of God and His promises, you embody the nature of a conqueror. The enemy no longer has the power to sink his claws into your heart, because you know Who you belong to. He is the one who goes before you and is behind you, surrounding you in the protection of His shadow.

As you experience suffering and feel yourself stepping into greater purpose as you learn more about God, do not allow yourself to be stuck in transition. When we pray to God, and when we ask Him for things, we have to be willing to allow wrecking balls to come into our lives. We have to be willing to embrace demolition and allow adversity to change our perspective. We have to be willing to get our feet wet, like the Old Testament priests did, if we want to truly feel the power of the Holy Spirit inside of us. The only way to change our perspective is through spending time with Him, in scripture and in prayer. We are able to step into our true purpose and heavenly calling when His promises become the foundation of our lives, and walking in faith becomes our primary mode of transportation.

I don't know where you are in your faith journey and your walk with Jesus, but every believer has the same constant need: to remind ourselves daily of God's promises. It's not only a reminder, but our livelihood. His promises create a new perspective in us, and this perspective governs our lifestyle. Everything is found in Him. Our walk with Him never has an end destination. I promise that if you continue to seek Him, you will never lose your awe of Him. There is never a dull moment with God. Once you allow Him to pour into you, He doesn't stop. That's when you start pouring onto others.

You realize that discipline and adversity is actually God's alignment of His will in your life. You start to look back and see why things happened the way they did; everything that has happened has led you to this moment. God's timing is perfect, and He waits patiently for every opportunity to set His face upon you when you turn towards Him. Don't take your eyes off Him. His promises fuel your mission and become your weapons against the attacks of the enemy. A bold, confident believer is dangerous to the enemy. Remember your stones, and remember the victory of the cross. I hope you can see that your mission is so much greater than yourself. It is such a privilege that God calls us to be part of His mission. Our mission—our purpose—is to lead others to the Promised Land, just as Joshua did.

Except this time, in this moment, our Promised Land is heaven. The best is yet to come.

PART 2: ASSIGNMENT

CALLING AND SPIRITUAL GIFTS

Somewhere within the pages of this book, God is calling your name. As we begin to discuss the ways God manifests Himself in your life, you will see how the alignment of His will and purpose is the catalyst to this transformational journey. This is made possible by accepting Jesus in your life so the Holy Spirit can begin to dwell in your heart. Consider His dwelling to be synonymous with manifestation. Other words for "manifestation" are *expression* and *demonstration;* the term *manifestation* is defined as "an event, action, or object that clearly shows or embodies something." I want to bring clarity to the New Age term referencing "manifestation." The New Age movement has muddied the term "manifestation" through this pagan, counterfeit philosophy that allows people to think that one is capable of creating their own reality, rather than trusting and obeying God, the only One capable of knowing and ordaining your future. In talking about "manifestation" in this book, I am referring to the physical demonstration and evidence to others that the Holy Spirit is active in your life and is working through you.

Your life is meant to be living proof that God is undeniably real and that the Holy Spirit lives in you. His goal is for you to align yourself with His will so He is able to manifest His Spirit within you to do incredible works through you. You are the catalyst for God to be able to illustrate his power to others. Remember, God told Paul, "My power is perfected in weakness."

This is why it is so important to understand Who our identity is tied to and why building our faith must be a priority in our lives. There is a reason we must first grow in spiritual maturity and continue to allow God to discipline us in His truths. In order to show others Who God is, we must know His heart first. Without building the basics, we don't have a solid foundation to stand on as we are called to boldly walk in God's purpose for our lives. God wants you to be confident in your purpose, not confused.

The purpose of God's alignment of His will over our lives is that gradually, He is transforming us to be more like Him and to be more sensitive to His voice. As we continue to journey with God and get closer to Him, what we see is that His will is actually becoming our will. His desires become our desires. The process that occurs as God manifests Himself in your life, and as He patiently and graciously teaches you what He wants to do through you, happens in the revelations that come to you as you spend time with Him. In other words, manifestation of God's presence and power in our lives become the evidence to others of exactly how God is working through us. We allow the Holy Spirit to shine through us, in our words and actions. The following chapters will break this down even further.

You cannot expect to love God and not be changed by Him. Although the storms may be destructive, you know He is always building it into something beautiful and impactful. Through your journey, walking hand in hand with God, you not only find strength and resilience, but also the ability to walk in confidence, knowing

He put you here to accomplish a heavenly purpose. God is wanting to use you in ways you can't even imagine.

Jesus gave you the key to discovering your true identity and unlocking your full potential. If you want to know how God wants to work through you, you need to know how to share this key with others. Remember, the Gospel is too good to keep to ourselves.

There are three key truths to unlock and embrace as God provides counsel and direction over our lives:

Calling: a continued process of surrender to learning how God wants to use you to carry out His work in the world.

Spiritual gifts: a unique, God-given ability that enables us to answer our calling according to His purpose.

Assignment: acting on God's divine instructions to carry out our heavenly mission and accomplish His will.

I pray that the following pages encourage you to press deeper into your relationship with God, and that the whisper of the Holy Spirit becomes the loudest voice in your life.

CHAPTER 10
LOVE LANGUAGE

There is nothing more powerful than the voice of God. It was His voice that spoke the entire universe into existence when He said, "Let there be light." In fact, all of scripture is God-breathed; He speaks to us through His written Word. It is His living, active message of hope to His children. I don't know about you, but if God's voice is able to speak an entire universe into existence, then it's definitely something worth listening to. One of the ways God speaks to us can be found through what Jesus did on the cross. If He died to save you and have a relationship with you, don't you think He wants to speak to you?

Discerning the voice of God is something we all must work on if we want to pursue His purpose for us and answer our calling. Listening to God and walking with God must go hand in hand. I'm not talking about an audible voice, either. It's that gentle nudge that encourages us to lean into Him. It's a quiet whisper that brushes the soft spot of our soul. His whisper may come across as a very distinct thought that's just a little bit higher than our own thinking. I believe

God whispers to us because in order to hear Him, we have to be quiet, and we have to be close.

There are many people, myself included, who have been in a season of life where we felt as if God was far away. We pray, and our prayers go unanswered. We pray for sickness to go away, and healing does not find us. We pray for depression and anxiety to leave us, and we can't seem to overcome our worry and stress. As much as God wants to speak to you, the enemy wants to just as much. At the end of the day, we must choose which we voice we listen to. Believe it or not, many of us listen to the voice of the enemy without even realizing it. One of the most valuable lessons we can learn as believers is to be able to discern the voice of God and the voice of the enemy. We talked about this in part 1 of this book, but let's dive deeper.

Our first divine assignment as children of God is to learn how to hear His voice. It makes sense; how can we answer our calling if we can't recognize His voice? Learning to do this allows us to build up a strong, discerning mind and heart. God wants to raise up people who have a heart in tune with His, because that is how He is most glorified. God is worthy of all glory, honor, and praise, and He works so people will be in awe of Him. That's why God loves turning impossible situations into mountain-moving miracles.

This was the Prophet Samuel's first assignment as the succeeding leader of Israel, after Eli's tenure. In those days, the Word of God and prophetic visions were very rare. Samuel was being called by God, but he didn't recognize His voice; he mistook it for Eli calling him. Eli had a heart in tune with God as well, and he realized that the voice Samuel was hearing was actually God. After three times of the Lord calling Samuel, and Samuel mistaking it for Eli, Eli instructed him to respond the next time God called him with, "Speak, Lord, for your servant is listening."

God called Samuel once more, and that was when Samuel finally recognized His voice. Once this happened, God spoke to Samuel, filling him with visions and prophecies, and because Samuel listened, he was able to act and speak in the ways God instructed him to.

Samuel became a leader, who had a heart for God, and who listened for His voice so he could develop a discerning spirit. Samuel became a leader because he submitted to listening for God's voice and acting on those instructions. God is able to accomplish so much through us when we submit to Him.

The issue that many of us struggle to grasp is that God does not have a speaking problem; we have a listening problem.

How many times have you prayed, and you were the one who did all the talking? Have you ever taken the time to just sit and be still in God's presence? Try to count the times you have said to God, "Speak, Lord, for your servant is listening." Many people lack wisdom and hinder their own spiritual growth because they don't take the time to listen to God and hear what He wants to say to them. The voice of God is all around us. He speaks to us through our pain, through people, and through communion with Him. The reason God wants a relationship with His children is because He desires a deep intimacy with us that the world is unable to give. When His children recognize a need for Him and pursue a keen ear for His whisper, that is when God is able to reveal the most wonderful heavenly treasures.

> Call to me and I will tell you great and incomprehensible things you do not know. (Jeremiah 33:3)

His whisper is His love language.

When you learn how to discern God's voice, you recognize there is a big difference between conviction and condemnation. Jesus made one thing very clear in His mission when He walked the earth. He said, "I did not come to judge the world but to save the world" (John 12:47).

God never stops pursuing you. You are either running from Him or running to Him. God uses conviction as a way to lovingly guide you back to Him. Conviction will have us confront ourselves, our sins, and unfortunately, the enemy will use condemnation as a way to make us feel either offended or unworthy of a relationship with God. I am here to tell you that the enemy is a liar.

Let me point something out you may not know. When Jesus came to earth, there was a reason that the type of people who were drawn to Him were those who were sick, broken, hurt, and lost. And there is also a reason Jesus was mocked and crucified at the hands of the "religious teachers," the Pharisees and lawmakers, those who proclaimed themselves to be righteous. The most "righteous people" were the ones who persecuted Jesus the most.

They thought that their self-righteousness was enough to save them. They didn't understand that what Jesus was about to do, lay down His life, was going to be the sacrifice needed for a grace that would save the world. Jesus said He didn't come to call the righteous; He came to call the sinners. He came to call the sick, the broken, the lost, the ones in need of healing, and the ones who have a heart that recognize a need for Him. That's how He works through us. Jesus changes everything. He desires for every single one of us to be a part of that. That's why people say God doesn't call the qualified; He qualifies the called.

You are called, but the key to maximum usefulness as a child of God and follower of Christ is that you must choose to answer your calling.

Sheep versus Goats

Now would be a good time to bring some clarity to a trend I've been seeing for a while now. You don't have to search far on the World Wide Web to see a lot of people being called "sheep" these days, as if to jokingly convey that people are mindlessly just following the herd. In other words, sheep (people) are compliant and will listen to whatever they're told. Society refers to people as sheep as a way to indicate they are ignorant and easily influenced. Sheep, by nature, are actually very docile. They're timid. They get frightened easily. They find protection from being in herds.

If you pay attention to scripture, you will see that today's society is very confused about what being a sheep actually means in a biblical context; people don't understand what Jesus said about sheep. When Jesus talked about sheep, He used it in parabolic form. As you already know, Jesus always taught in parables. I know you've heard people refer to Jesus as our Shepherd. In fact, Jesus said that His sheep (referring to His children) follow Him because they know His voice.

> The sheep follow Him because they know His voice. They will never follow a stranger; instead they will run away from him, because they don't know the voice of strangers. (John 10:4–5)

Jesus said this because he actually knew how incredibly smart sheep are. I don't know if you know this, but sheep (in real life) only recognize and come to their master's voice. Look it up. YouTube it. Type in, "Sheep Know Shepherd's Voice." What you'll find is the sheep, when called by a stranger, do not acknowledge the voice at all. They won't even lift their heads. They ignore the stranger's voice. But when their shepherd calls them, every single sheep lifts their head and follows the voice. When Jesus spoke in parables, he not only spoke actual truth, he also spoke heavenly truth. Sheep are actually incredibly intelligent animals. They only follow the voice of their master, their shepherd. That's the only voice they trust.

Jesus refers to us as His sheep, because He knows that once we begin a relationship with Him and learn how to discern His voice, His voice becomes the only one we know and trust. As we grow in spiritual maturity and learn how to depend on God, His Holy Spirit becomes our inner compass. We recognize the difference between our Shepherd's voice and the enemy's voice; we know which one provides, and we know which one divides.

It says in Matthew chapter 25 that when Jesus returns in all of His glory and with all of His angels, He will separate the people from one another, just as the shepherd separates the sheep from the goats. It says, "He will put the sheep on His right and the goats on

His left." You don't want to be on the left. Goats are referred to in the Bible as those who do not know Jesus.

Just as much as society ridicules people for being sheep, there is also a trend where people call others the "GOAT," which is an acronym for Greatest Of All Time. People refer to all of these celebrities, athletes, rappers, and idols as the GOAT. We glamorize, celebrate, and glorify these people by calling them the GOAT.

The intent may be harmless; however, the enemy is a carefully calculated and deceitful liar, who will do anything to twist God's truths to make it trendy or culturally acceptable. When you read the Word of God, you are much more aware of when society, and the principles of the Bible, are complete opposite. It would be disobedience to not call it out.

Jesus says one thing about sheep and goats; the world says another.

This is just an example of why we need discernment, and why we must be in tune for listening for God's voice above all else. We want to be sheep. We want to follow the voice that is sure to lead us to heavenly pastures. Biblical clarity is key for navigating the confusion of this world. It is a gift and a privilege to follow God, our Shepherd. The voice of God is the most necessary component of our walk with Him. God calls His people to follow Him all throughout scripture. We can witness the blessings that result from obedience, as well as the consequences of disobedience.

We can follow the world, or we can follow God, but we can't do both. The choice ultimately depends on which voice we choose to listen to.

The Enemy's Worst Nightmare

The biggest spiritual pandemic is that there are so many of us who are walking through life, not realizing our full potential and not truly understanding the power we have as children of God. This is why it is so important to continue to remind one another of our true identity in Christ. Jesus says in Luke 10:19, "Look, I have given you the authority to trample on snakes and scorpions and over all the power of the enemy; nothing at all will harm you."

Jesus wasn't talking about actual snakes and scorpions; He was talking about the spiritual warfare we have with the enemy. Don't forget that your true identity means you are able to act and walk in the authority of our Savior. In other words, God gives us power over the enemy. Have you ever thought about the fact that God is big enough to fill the heavens and the heart of every believer, and yet the enemy is small enough to fit underneath our feet?

That is the type of authority I am talking about.

However, there is a level of fear, worry, doubt, and anxiety that hinders us from being who God is calling us to be. We don't feel good enough; we don't feel like God can use someone like us; we've sinned too much. We need to understand that God's grace is bigger than all of our sins. Jesus's sacrifice removed the penalty of sin in our lives, so we don't have to live as slaves to sin anymore. Because He removed the penalty of sin, this also means we are free from the power of sin over our lives. We are free to live in anticipation of heaven, because His grace covers us. We must stop feeling inadequate and start allowing God into our hearts so we can listen for that voice that tells us how He wants to use us to help others.

We know that our salvation is secured the moment we confess with our mouth and believe in our heart that Jesus Christ is our Lord and Savior; once you start a relationship with Him, nothing can take that away from you. There is no sin that can take that away from you. However, the moment you start a relationship with Jesus, you are going to spend the rest of your life with a permanent target on your back.

I'm going to let you in on a little secret the enemy doesn't want you to know: The devil knows you've been saved. He knows your salvation is secured. He knows he can't take it away. Jesus said it Himself: "I give them eternal life, and they will never perish. No one will snatch them out of my hand" (John 10:28).

The devil can't touch you. There is no one who is able to stand toe-to-toe with God Almighty. God's got you. Knowledge of that truth alone is how people are able to be bold and unashamed of the Gospel.

> If God is for us, who is against us? (Romans 8:31)

The answer is no one. Let me hit you with another biblical headline:

> You are from God, little children, and you have conquered them, because the one who is in you is greater than the one who is in the world. (1 John 4:4)

The One Who is in you is the Holy Spirit. As long as you have a target on your back, the enemy is going to throw darts at you. You better believe it. The enemy doesn't sleep. It's invaluable for believers to know the enemy's motives and schemes. So let me remind you once more that when the voice of fear, guilt, worry, doubt, or shame creep up in your mind, you need to know that those thoughts/emotions are not from God, and if they're not from God, they are lies.

We must recognize these battles for what they are if we are going to answer God's calling for our lives and walk in our purpose. The enemy is going to keep throwing darts and feeding you with those lies because you are a threat to his mission to seek, kill, and destroy. If you are saved by the blood of Jesus: You. Are. A. Threat.

Since the enemy knows he can't take your salvation away, he's going to pull out his big guns and do everything he can to keep you cowering under those lies and deceitful emotions, to tempt you into believing those lies, so you don't feel worthy enough to answer your calling and walk in your heavenly mission to bring others to Jesus. He can't take your salvation away, but he sure can try to keep you from walking in your purpose. He works hard in the spirit of depression to dim your God-given light to this world. If the enemy can keep believers from pursuing their mission, walking in their true power under the crown of God Almighty and sharing the good news of the Gospel and planting the seeds, then he gets the victory in those battles. We can't let the enemy win, especially when we have a Savior Who already has. The truth is our power.

You see, the enemy doesn't fear the nonbelievers. Those are easy targets for him. The enemy fears the ones who have a Holy Spirit dwelling inside of them, submitted to pursuing their heavenly mission above all else, being all that God has called them to be. The enemy's biggest fear and worst nightmare is the moment submitted believers step into their true power and voice, with a mission to help build up the Kingdom of God. The enemy does not want you to know the power you have as a child of God. That's why Jesus said you have the authority to trample on the enemy. You have the power to stomp on those lies. I want to be clear that the enemy doesn't make you do anything, but he will tempt you and exhaust you and tempt you into giving in to those lies or giving in to sin. But once you are able to discern the voice of God from the voice of the enemy, once you figure out exactly how the devil works, you will be able to act in the authority of our King and keep your foot on the devil's throat.

Being a child of God is your superpower.

That is why we must stay in the Word. That is our source of strength. That is our instruction manual for learning how to tune our heart to the voice of God. There is no shortcut. Time spent with Him is how the Holy Spirit manifests inside of us in such a way that it builds and stirs within us. If you continue to invest in your relationship with Him, I promise you, He stirs you up, and that Word is like a match that will set your soul on fire, to the point that you are just burning to teach others the Gospel and show people Who Jesus is.

It is equally important to tell people Who Jesus is, just as much as it is to show them Who Jesus is, and we can't do that if we haven't strengthened our minds and hearts to be able to withstand the enemy's attacks and deceitful mind games. The enemy's voice is loud;

it is so easy for our minds to be consumed with fear and anxiety. The voice of God is soft and quiet, because in order for us to hear Him, we must be still, lean in, and intentionally listen for Him.

The enemy knows that God hides lions inside of lambs. I pray that God uses this generation to fill His children up with a mighty roar that breaks strongholds, makes evil flee and brings to light the beauty, power and freedom that comes from a relationship with Him. I pray for revival. I pray that God is using this season and this book to bring up believers who are unashamed and unafraid to roar for the Kingdom of God. It is our love language to speak the truth to others, no matter how hard or uncomfortable it may be. The Holy Spirit is the lion inside of you.

Never forget that as a child of God, you are a force and a threat to the enemy.

Roar.

CHAPTER 11
A KINGDOM MINDSET

> For although we live in the flesh, we do not wage war according to the flesh, since the weapons of our warfare are not of the flesh, but are powerful through God for the demolition of strongholds. (2 Corinthians 10:3–4)

This world is a spiritual war zone. There is no escaping it. We live in the midst of a battle between good and evil, and as children of God, we have the tools and power to overcome evil with good. I can't stress this enough. This is what Paul tried to teach people in his letters to the churches in New Testament scripture. Paul was giving them instructions on how to stand strong in their faith and how to develop the correct mindset necessary to carry out their assignment in this world.

A Kingdom mindset is rooted in our mission: to lead people to Jesus, in hopes to bring as many people to heaven with us as possible. The mission is the same for every follower of Christ: to plant seeds as we preach the truth of the Gospel and to show people Who our Savior is. It's to bring the intimate persona of Christ and exuberant joy of heaven to earth, so others can not only hear what we have to say, but see our love and joy for God Almighty as well. This is the type of unity and peace the world is so desperately searching for.

We all have the same mission; it's our assignments that will look different. Grasping this Kingdom mindset will also help you better understand your assignment. Your assignment is rooted in your unique expression of God to those around you. Your assignment is rooted in your passions and spiritual gifts, which we will discuss later.

Our mission has Kingdom purpose, and our assignment is our influence.

There is a lot to unpack in order to truly bring understanding to what it means to have a Kingdom mindset. This mentality is something many believers never quite seem to grasp, but it's so crucial to fulfilling our mission as ambassadors for Christ; it can only be discovered as you learn God's will for your life and surrender to it, and learn to discern the inner voice of the Holy Spirit. This mentality is necessary in order to follow Jesus; it's a boldness that blossoms through learning our true identity and developing an unshakable faith that enables us to step in confidence as we follow Him, planting seeds of truth.

Developing a Kingdom mindset is a part of the process of surrender that we discussed in part 1. Let me start off by saying that this mindset is a permanent attitude, governed by God's will, purpose, and plans, that determines in advance how we will respond to people and situations. It is a mindset that responds with faith, rather than reacts with emotion. It is a mindset that strives for obedience and desires wisdom from God. It is a mindset that thinks and believes with a higher level of conviction, because your thoughts are ruled by heavenly things, not earthly things. This mentality is built through an imperishable hope in the promises of God.

This is why the discipline of God's truths and resting in

His promises are prerequisites to building the foundation of this mentality. Allowing the promises of God to take root in your heart is essential to truly understanding, embracing, and embodying the person God has called you to be. A Kingdom mindset begins with understanding and believing that God has called you and set you apart for a very special purpose, followed with the daily choice to answer His calling and seek His will to be done above your own fleshly desires.

The secret is not in our bravery to pursue God and our heavenly mission; the secret is in His power. A Kingdom mindset is when you allow the Holy Spirit to control your thoughts, your tongue, and your actions. People were able to see miracles from God first-hand when Jesus walked the earth. The reason we say Jesus is still alive is because His Holy Spirit dwells inside of us. We represent Him. People are still able to witness the power of God today because it is His followers, His ambassadors, who testify to His miracles and glorify Him. It's a permanent Philippians 4:13 outlook on life: "I am able to do all things through him who strengthens me."

Just as God can only work in a heart that recognizes a need for Him, He can only work through a heart that desires to glorify Him.

This is why it is so important that we are taking time to make sure we are surrendering to God's will and seeking Him first, so we can understand how He is aligning our lives according to His will. Jesus said in Matthew 6:33, "Seek first the Kingdom of God and His righteousness." This is so we are disciplined and trained to better understand how we are supposed to represent the Kingdom. We are proclaimed righteous through our faith in Jesus Christ, not by our works. A Kingdom mindset is understanding that God looks at us through the eyes of our Savior, Who cleansed us from our sins with His blood. It is through faith and repentance that we commit our lives to following Him and continue the process of surrender by allowing God to train us to think more like Him and be more like Him. We cannot be effective ambassadors of Christ if our actions and thoughts aren't in line with His perspective, will, desires, and plans.

It took me thirty years to understand that I am called, and I have a purpose. Not only understand it, but truly live by my calling and walk in my purpose. It took all this time for me to finally understand that the end of my life here on earth is just the beginning of eternity with Jesus, and that the ultimate goal is to bring as many people to heaven as I possibly can, with the borrowed time I have here.

The years weren't wasted, though. God has been carefully and strategically ordaining my steps to lead me to Him. He's been aligning the trials of my life to teach me to depend on Him fully and so He could reveal Himself to me in ways I didn't even know were possible. These years were the preparation and alignment I needed in order to see things from His perspective. I spent all that time asking God to change my circumstances, rather than asking Him to use my circumstances to change me. Once that Kingdom mindset became mature enough to understand how God was building my faith, it was game over for the enemy. I understand now that God has been training me my whole life to become a warrior for His Kingdom. I'm working in my assignment now. His mission is now my mission. I finally understand that building this Kingdom mindset is why the enemy works so hard to distract us and discourage us, to keep us from understanding.

Once we realize this, we also understand that as God's children, we have the authority to keep the enemy under our feet, because that's just how small he really is compared to our God.

The enemy knows you can't break people who get their strength from God, and that is why God is so desperately after your heart. Once He has your heart, the Holy Spirit can begin to manifest inside you, to empower and strengthen you. The Holy Spirit is our counsel. It is the voice that lovingly directs our thoughts and hearts. It's a voice that you feel. That's why I say it's so important to recognize where the source of your thoughts come from. We see multiple times in scripture that people were filled with the Holy Spirit, led by the Holy Spirit, or sent out by the Holy Spirit. Once we begin a relationship with Jesus, we are inviting Him and the Holy Spirit to reside and dwell in our hearts so He is able to work through us. Focus on the relationship. Focus on Him, and allow Him to guide you and direct your steps.

Wherever you find yourself right now, your years weren't wasted, either. If you woke up today, God isn't finished with you, and His timing is always perfect. In other words, God never wastes time, because everything that happens in our lives is according to His heavenly clock. Maybe this book is God's way of calling you to take your relationship with Him to another level. God is not in the business of stagnation and complacency; He is in the business of spiritual growth and maturity. God never wants to stop His good work in you, which is why He simply needs a willing heart that desires to learn and advance the heavenly agenda. This was Paul's prayer for spiritual growth, and this is what I pray for you today:

> We are asking [God] that you may be filled with the knowledge of his will in all wisdom and spiritual understanding, so that you may walk worthy of the Lord, fully pleasing to Him: bearing fruit in every good work and growing in the knowledge of God, being strengthened with all power, according to his glorious might, so that you may have great endurance and patience, joyfully giving thanks to the Father, who has enabled you to share in the saints' inheritance in the light. He has rescued us from the domain of darkness and transferred us into the kingdom of the Son he loves. In him we have redemption, the forgiveness of sins. (Colossians 1:9–14)

The word *Kingdom* is referenced in the New Testament 154 times, and Jesus used the term ninety-three times. We know by now that when Jesus spoke, it got people's attention. That's why the New Testament is full of Jesus's teachings and parables. His disciples were convicted to write it down. So if He speaks about something ninety-three times in scripture, I believe it is worth paying attention to. God brought heaven down to earth so He could not only be a living sacrifice for us, but so we could receive Him and represent His Kingdom, celebrating, worshipping, and sharing the truths that encourage those around us to see what being in a relationship with God looks like. We are His Kingdom of believers now, eagerly waiting for His Kingdom soon to come.

The Kingdom of God is both a destination and a mindset.

Heavenly Citizenship

Another piece of the permanent attitude God wants us to have is that He wants us to live in anticipation of being with Him for eternity in heaven. The apostle Paul put it this way: "If we have put our hope in Christ for this life only, we should be pitied more than anyone" (1 Corinthians 15:19).

He didn't say this to condemn anyone or make people feel guilty. He said this so people could grasp the full nature of what it means to hope in our future in heaven, which also allows us to put our trials in perspective. If our hope is tied to life here, and not in what's to come when we get to heaven, then we don't have the right mindset. If we want God to use us, we must understand that the rope of our hope is anchored in His Word and tied to heaven.

If you want to read about what we have to look forward to, as well as grow in the knowledge of God, I strongly encourage you to read 1 and 2 Peter. His whole purpose behind writing those books was to encourage believers that we can live with an unshakable confidence that we will be in God's presence one day very soon. What's interesting about Peter's message is that he is writing these books in the midst of his own suffering and persecution. He was an eyewitness to the life and death of Jesus, and encouraged the members of the church to endure suffering and pursue righteousness in the midst of a very hostile world.

As believers, there is no other option but to persevere in our faith. Peter's encouragement to us today is the same encouragement he gave to his people; recognize trouble as only temporary, and secure your hope in what is eternal. Our Kingdom mindset must be rooted in eternity. We can rest assured that we are on the winning side. We have the promises of God that will never fail us.

> But based on his promise, we wait for new heavens and a new earth, where righteousness dwells. (2 Peter 3:13)

Let these truths sit on your heart. Soak them in. Meditate on them. Your citizenship is a part of your identity. It's not just whose you are, but where you belong. We belong with God. He is looking forward to the day He gets to bring you home to heaven, but until that day comes, you have breath and life for a reason. God has planned our redemption since the beginning of time. We aren't of this world, so we must not think or act like this world. We are called to be different. We are called to follow God, and we can't follow God and the world at the same time. We must choose. We must pick up our cross daily and follow Him. Taking up our cross means stretching our faith so it can grow.

This walk with God is not just reserved for Sunday mornings. God didn't carve out Sundays as the only day for a weekly appointment with Him. That's not how relationships work, and it's most definitely not how God works. He wants our hearts consumed with Him because He knows the benefits we have when we do; it sets our hearts on fire for Him. We should be using each day to grow closer to Him and build our faith. If we want to understand and mature in our mindset, our relationship with God must be an intentional, daily pursuit. The only way to lead people to Jesus is by following Him.

Think Like a Child

Never once in the Bible does God refer to us as His "adults." We are called God's children, because He is our Father in heaven. Jesus actually spent a lot of time with children, and you can read in the Gospel of Luke that He taught a parable to His disciples about what it means to become like children in our ways of thinking. I know that might sound contradictory to this entire chapter and the task of maturing in our mindset as followers of Christ, but this is another very important piece of the permanent attitude God wants us to have.

> Truly I tell you, whoever does not receive the kingdom of God like a little child will never enter it. (Luke 18:17)

We all know several things about the mind of a child: Their brains are sponges, they have absolutely no filter, and they love to ask questions.

Let me be clear that God does not expect us to be juvenile in our thinking. But notice how Jesus doesn't talk about achieving the Kingdom. He doesn't insinuate that any effort is needed at all. He talks about receiving the Kingdom as a way to teach His disciples that the Kingdom is yours to receive, but it's only possible to do so if you approach your relationship with Him the same way a child would: 1) with a heart like a sponge, ready and open to receive and accept His truths, 2) coming to Him exactly as you are (#nofilter), and 3) with questions ready, ears willing to listen, and a mind eager to learn.

Let me give you an example.

Children cannot do anything themselves. They are helpless, dependent, and needy. Their parents are responsible for disciplining them and guiding them as they grow up. Children also have not yet learned to rationalize truth and think logically; they need their parent to do that for them, and children ultimately trust that they are being taken care of. They believe what their parents tell them. Children are also very inquisitive and always asking questions, because intellectually, they are always in a constant posture to learn.

This is how we are in relation to our Father in heaven. As children of God, we rely completely on Him to take care of us, meet our needs, and put faith in our salvation in Him. We never lose the need to depend entirely on God. We never grow up into adults; we are always His children. Unless we are able to put humility in front of our pride and admit the need for Him and receive Him in our lives, we are not able to receive the eternal Kingdom of God, as well as the enlightenment to the treasures and truths of the Gospel.

Think back to chapter 7, "Functional Faith." Remember the little girl who asked Jesus to heal her, and when He did, she believed it was because of Him, without a fraction of a doubt? The confidence of her faith is an example of what it means to have a Kingdom mindset.

That's why the mind of a child is so precious. When we teach our children about God, they fully embrace it and believe it as truth. I know of other children who have witnessed to others about Jesus. The Holy Spirit speaks through children. It's not until we grow into adulthood that the stressors of life and the development of rational thinking causes us to do more questioning. It's not a bad thing to have questions, but it's spiritual cataclysm to question things without the development of our faith and trust in God Almighty.

Like children, we must cling to the cross like children do to their parent's leg.

Patience Is a Virtue

A lot of times we find ourselves asking God, if He really is as good as He says He is, then why does He allow so many bad things to happen in this world? Why doesn't God just snap His mighty fingers and put an end to it?

Scripture has an answer for those questions, too.

2 Peter 3:15 tells us to "regard the patience of our Lord as salvation."

Before God allowed for the destruction of the Holy Temple in Jerusalem, He waited a very long time for the people to repent and follow Him. Today, God is still waiting for people to turn to Him, because just as God exiled His people out of the holy city of Jerusalem, there will come a day where God will permanently exile His people to an eternal life in hell. Hell is only for those who never accepted the gift of grace and salvation, and received Jesus Christ as their Savior.

Peter also goes on to say, "The Lord does not delay his promise, as some understand delay, but is patient with you, not wanting any to perish but all to come to repentance" (2 Peter 3:9).

One thing about God is that it is not in His will to send anyone to hell. If you want to know why there is so much ugliness and hatefulness in this world, it's not because He necessarily allows it, but it's because our God will move mountains and shake the earth to get your attention. He cannot take away our free will, but He will move heaven and earth to get your attention so you will repent and turn to Him. Free will is what gives us the choice to accept or reject that Jesus Christ's sacrifice on the cross was sufficient to save every single one of us.

This is why God desires for His followers to take an active approach in following Him, and push the Kingdom agenda in this world. We are the hands and feet of God, relying on Him, His Word, and His instructions to tell us how He wants us to impact the world and bring glory to Him. The world is full of too many apathetic Christians who have become complacent and passive in their relationship with God, and as a result, they make accommodations to the world and things that are not of God, when they should actually be calling them out. It is up to us to show people Who Jesus is, and it is also up to us to call out the darkness and evil in this world. The way to conquer evil is by bringing the truth to light.

Light exposes darkness.

> If we say, "We have fellowship with him," and yet we walk in darkness, we are lying and not practicing the truth. (1 John 1:6)

God wants all of His children to know Him, love Him, and be with Him in heaven when the time comes. Each day we are given is a miracle. Let's not waste the opportunity to use each day to plant seeds of truth. I am so thankful that God has been patient with me and did not cut my days short before I decided to turn to Him and accept Him in my life. Many of us can look back and be thankful that God was faithful to us, even during the days that we were far from Him and didn't know Him. Unfortunately, there are many people in this world who cannot say that. So while we are here, we must pursue our heavenly mission and allow God to work in our hearts so He can work through us in our heavenly assignments. There are too many lost souls who need to see the light we are walking in. Let's pray for God to help us understand patience the same way He does.

God has a plan to reach people in this world, and you and I are an important part of that plan. He's already chosen us; He's just patiently waiting on us to choose Him.

CHAPTER 12
LIVING IN THE TENSION

Jesus said that "a loveless world is a sightless world."

In other words, a world devoid of love is like the blind leading the blind. The world is desperate to see peace and unity, especially in the time we are living in now.

The hardest thing a Christian is tasked with is trying to share the love of Christ and be bold for the Kingdom, in a world that continues to be moving in the opposite direction of God. We are called to stand for the truth in a world that is blinded by darkness. Darkness is driven by the evil forces in this world. We know evil is sin, and sin keeps people in the darkness. It's a vicious cycle that we want so badly to end. We want evil, hate, injustice, and corruption to stop. We want the world to live in harmony, yet we see it continue to move in a direction that is further and further away from the solution. The world is in a crisis. We live in a society that is divided on disagreements. We dislike, unfriend, and even dismantle the character of people who see the world differently and have different perspectives than us. Differences and disagreement are becoming even more personal, and people lash out at each other behind a keyboard on a daily basis. If I'm being honest, I see many Christians today who seem more concerned with winning arguments than winning hearts.

The reason people get so upset about the things going on in this world is because we know, deep down, that it's not supposed to be this way. Every issue in today's society is so quickly consumed by political agendas, and the topics are used to fit different narratives and opinions. This world has never known peace. Unfortunately, this world will never know peace. The type of hope, unity, and peace we wish to see will never be found in this world.

However, there is a day coming soon when Jesus will return to bring His heavenly Kingdom. He is going to make everything new, where peace, unity, and righteousness will dwell and be everlasting. It will be a happily ever after, forever. Our Savior tells us to share this good news with others. But until that day comes, we have a job to do, and our job must involve a much higher level of thinking and perspective that rises above the darkness of this world, so we know how to think, act, and teach others about our Savior, Who is coming back one day soon. This is where the Kingdom mindset plays such a huge role in our lives. This mindset puts the darkness of this world into perspective. We live victoriously because we know that in the end, light will overcome darkness. We know how the story ends. Love will win because it already has. Love won the day Jesus took His last breath and said, "It is finished."

I am not trying to dismiss or ignore the realities of the current state of our world. But through a relationship with Jesus, He lovingly puts the realities of this world into perspective and shows us how to live in the tensions of society, working through us to help others discover where our hope is rooted and navigate their way to heaven. There has never been a more important time for people to know Jesus. He is the only hope we have, and thankfully, He is the only hope we need. But we must be careful with the world's lost souls. The world's lost souls are usually the ones who tend to offend us the most; the ones we don't like. As I mentioned before, sometimes, the only way people come to know Jesus is if they are treated with the same grace Jesus gives us every day. We are the flavor of our Savior, and we represent His Kingdom everywhere we go.

Now is the time to walk boldly in the Word of God and for His Kingdom. There are so many people who have been saved, but they don't have the Word planted in their heart. We must continue to take the time to nurture and grow our roots in Him. This is why we must make a choice every single day to allow God's voice to be the loudest one in our lives. When we do, we are a force. When we don't, we are bogged down with the enemy's lies. The enemy knows a Kingdom divided cannot stand.

Look around. Division is all around us. Do you see what the enemy is doing? Our hearts are being polluted with division and distractions. And we know by now that both of those things are the enemy's main methods to adding more darkness to this world.

Spiritual warfare is so real, and we are part of "Operation No Souls Left Behind." We have to help our world understand where they can find hope. We must keep our eyes on Jesus.

Before we go any further, I want to add a short disclaimer that this is the chapter of the book that will probably make you feel most uncomfortable.

And I hope it does. Honestly, if this chapter doesn't make you feel at least a tad bit uncomfortable, then I don't believe I'm doing a good job at explaining the sobering truth of the need for the Kingdom call to action we all have, as the underlying purpose and mission for our lives. Also, because as you continue to read, if you begin to feel uncomfortable and uneasy, I believe it's the Holy Spirit's way of using His convicting ways to stir up a fire in your heart, designed to help you understand how you must discover your purpose, and shift your perspective on your role as an ambassador for the Kingdom.

I ask that you allow conviction to do its work in your heart. There is a very deep level of thinking I want you to do so you can not only understand my intentions within the pages of these words, but also lift the veil on what God may be wanting to say to you. This book is not going to let you settle for mediocre truth, because that's not how God works. We don't serve a mediocre God, by any means. I believe one of the biggest reasons the Bible often gets mislabeled as hateful or offensive is because its truths are very inconvenient to the lifestyles we live. We cherry-pick the parts of the Bible that make us feel good, rather than allow conviction to do its work and hold us accountable for the areas of our heart we must work on ourselves. The world and watered-down churches will sugarcoat sin, to make people feel more comfortable, or like they're not as bad as other sinners.

Too often, we settle in mediocre truth, in what's comfortable. But comfortable doesn't push us to be who God created us to be. Our calling is not found in our comfort zones. The world will continue to mistake truth for hate, because nothing about the truths in the Bible are convenient or comfortable.

The only thing we should be comfortable with is resting in the fact that Jesus died a death that we deserved to die. He took the punishment we deserved. It is through Him that we are able to rest in knowing that life after death is our future, which we get to look forward to in anticipation and joy. We have to get comfortable with being uncomfortable if we truly want to walk in our purpose and be obedient to God's calling for our lives. Living a life obedient to Christ will have you living outside your comfort zone, and this is something scripture tells us to be prepared for. But the one thing we can't do, as followers of Christ, is compromise the truth or His Word, for the sake of not offending people.

Unfortunately, people often mistake God's truth as offensive, because many people (myself included) have been hurt by the church; they've felt condemnation from church members. People don't want to hear about or trust Jesus because their opinion of Jesus is based on how they've already been treated by others. Believers in Christ are how other people experience Jesus. I cannot express that enough.

And one of the hardest things to do as a Christian is stand in the middle of the tensions of society and exemplify the true character of Jesus. It's a very fine line to walk, because God says that the righteous are bold, and He also says that we are to give grace to others, just as He gives grace to us. As I've journeyed through this walk with Christ, those instructions have often created turmoil within me, and that's something I've had to lean into with God, through stillness and prayer.

How do I stand up for the Kingdom and His truths, but at the same time, do so with a tender, gentle heart? How do I be bold, yet compassionate? How do I remain humble, yet assertive? How do I speak with a heart of conviction, rather than a heart of condemnation?

I don't know if anyone has ever told you this, but it is not a sin to ask questions. When you ask questions with a heart eager to listen, God will point you in the direction of the answers He desires to reveal to you. You may have the same questions as me. This is also why, in order to be able to live in the tensions of society and deal with conflict and division in this world the way followers of Christ are supposed to, you must be ready to discern the direction and voice that only the Holy Spirit can give to you. I will be the first to tell you that we must be listening to that voice that tells us how to respond and not react.

When Jesus commissioned His disciples, He knew what kind of battle they were up against, so He gave them instructions on how to deal with the tension and handle the weight of persecution so many Christians face today.

> Jesus said, "I am sending you out like sheep among wolves. Therefore be as shrewd as serpents and as innocent as doves." (Matthew 10:16)

I would be doing you a great injustice if I didn't use this opportunity to point you in the direction of the words from an incredible author, civil rights activist, and follower of Christ: Martin Luther King Jr. (MLKJ). Jesus knew what He was asking of His disciples, and of you and I, today. Jesus is well aware of the fact that this world is full of evil and people are persecuted because of the love we have for Christ. MLKJ best explains Jesus's instructions by writing that "we must combine the toughness of the serpent and the softness of the dove, a tough mind and a tender heart" (King, 2).

To be shrewd, means to show a clever awareness; to be tough-minded. I interpret a dove-like innocence as being full of the things that make us compassionate in character, like peace, love, gentleness, and purity. When Jesus was telling His disciples to be both of those at the same time, the way I understand it is that tough-mindedness, to be sharp and discerning, comes from knowing, and understanding, and being rooted in truth; being rooted in the Word. Tender-heartedness comes from knowing, and understanding, and being rooted in the character and nature of Jesus. God calls us to have both theological backbones of steel as well as a cultivated heart of compassion and grace.

In other words, we must be tough-minded and disciplined enough to discern godly wisdom from what's happening in this world, as well as the enemy's schemes. God knows that we can only do this through a relationship with Him and a willingness to pursue heavenly truths. Those truths will help us cultivate a tender heart, which comes through understanding Christ's character and His capacity to love and forgive. Embracing His character is how we understand our identity in Him. This perspective is required of us if we are to live and love the way God expects us to.

This world is waiting on others to love first. We have this unspoken mentality that in order for us to love, it must be given first. That's not how Jesus showed us how it works, though. The love Jesus gave was not contingent on reciprocity. In fact, people hated Him because of the love He gave. He gave it anyway. This is why He must use us as the vessel to reach others, to show the world what it means and looks like to be wrapped in His truth and grace. The world needs people, and God is calling us, to stand in the middle of conflict and absorb the tensions of this world with grace, truth, and light.

This is why we must get used to being uncomfortable in order for God to use us, because I believe that as Christians, as followers of Jesus Christ, we are purposefully placed in this world, in the middle of the tension, corruption, and brokenness, so we can act as a filter for deciphering the harsh realities of this world by transforming them into purpose, life-giving truth, and direction. And while we are in the middle, we should be the filter and the lens, to magnify Christ in everything we do and say, as well as magnifying Him to deliver truths when the enemy puts in overtime to deceive and deter people from a relationship with Jesus.

Living in the tension is exactly where believers are called to be.

Human beings are on a quest, for righteousness to triumph. So were the early Jewish people of Israel. Everything about their world was corrupted with evil and injustice. They were waiting on a Messiah to come and conquer and fix everything. When Jesus showed up, a thirty-year-old carpenter from Nazareth, He wasn't exactly what they had in mind on how their Messiah should look and act. So when He announced Himself as their promised Messiah, teaching others about the Kingdom, the people hated Him for it, accusing Him of blasphemy.

Jesus came to show those who were eager to listen that being a follower of Christ is not for the strong, proud, and loud; it is for the weak, gentle, and humble. That is what the Jewish lawmakers and high priests didn't understand about the Messiah. Jesus's heavenly mission was so much more than what they were willing to open their minds and hearts to. Jesus was a King, yet He acted with a servant mentality. He was tough-minded and tender-hearted at the same time, always showing us how to be that example for others, and how to live among the chaos and tension in this world. The Word of God is wisdom, and the heart of God is grace. It is my own personal speculation that they envisioned their promised Savior to be tough-minded and cold-hearted, with the way they anticipated justice to be served. Aren't we glad God doesn't always give us what we ask for?

The way we are supposed to treat and love others is not going to be understood by those who have yet to accept Jesus Christ and invite the Holy Spirit in their lives; that's why your faith will often be challenged by others. But we are called to live a life very different from the rest of the world. We are called to be the light, at all costs, in a very broken and dark world. We're not fighting a battle of humanity against humanity; it's not us versus them. It's good versus evil. We are fighting a battle within a spiritual realm that we cannot see. The enemy is not people. It's so easy to get frustrated because we see and experience injustice, corruption, and betrayal every day.

But understand this:

People live in darkness and love darkness because they have been lied to, manipulated, and deceived by Satan himself. Evil is not an illusion; our real enemy is not another person or the government. The only way to truly change the hearts of people is by driving out hate with the light we have because we've been saved by grace in Jesus's name. As believers, we must understand that it's a spiritual battle of God's children versus the enemy. We are His soldiers who fight with a different type of sword. If we are able to gain that perspective, the devil doesn't stand a fighting chance in this world.

We are far from perfect, and we are not expected to be, but God's love most certainly is. As long as we can show up for God and love people the way we are supposed to, then God will take care of the rest. He will transform their hearts, because that's His job. We are simply just helping direct traffic, planting seeds of truth along the way, until we are called to our heavenly home. The law of love is not something that can be passed through an act of Congress. There are no laws that will legislate love in our country. Our hearts must be convicted before perpetuators of corruption and injustice.

It takes more strength to hate than it does to love. It takes more strength to retaliate than it does to forgive. And if you feel that it takes more strength to do the opposite of the two, to love and forgive, then you might want to check the condition of your heart. If we want to be a true follower and accomplish our heavenly mission in this world, while we're still here, we must strive to make sure our thoughts, words, and actions align with Jesus's character, no matter what. MLKJ, a true contender for unity, also had some wise words to say about love and this thing called "unenforceable obligations."

Love, the weapon for personal and social transformation, can only be achieved by true neighbors who are willingly obedient to unenforceable obligations; unenforceable obligations are beyond the reach of the laws of society. They concern inner attitudes, genuine person-to-person relations, and expressions of compassion that law books cannot regulate and jails cannot rectify. We must admit that the solutions to the problem lie in the willingness of people to obey the unenforceable (King, 28–30).

What does that mean?

It's an invisible law that means godly love. Hate the sin, love the sinner. Love does not mean you are blind to the sins of the world, but it changes your response to sin. The solution involves a love that is not tied to offense or emotional circumstances. Love is a real action that stems from an eternal love that God has, so that by knowing Him, we are able to show grace to others so people understand what that godly love looks like. That is how we become world-changers. God doesn't call us to love with stipulations. He says to leave the wrath up to Him and love regardless. His love has the power to unify, and it always wins.

> Above all, put on love, which is the perfect bond of unity. (Colossians 3:14)

Contending for Unity

I want to highlight a person in the Bible who wanted unity and justice for his people in the worst way: Jeremiah.

Jeremiah was one of the greatest prophets in the Old Testament, and he was called into ministry at a very young age. Jeremiah felt for people. He lived during a time where he witnessed acts of injustice and evil, but he also had a very strong relationship with God. You are able to see this for yourself if you read the book of Jeremiah, which is full of his conversations with God and his accounts of what was happening in the world around him at the time.

To give you a little historical context, Jeremiah grew up in a village a few miles outside the city of Jerusalem, and if you didn't know, Jerusalem had a reputation known for God's name. It still does to this day. God had done incredible things for the people, and His Holy Temple was established in Jerusalem. However, the people did not follow God. They felt that their holy city was untouchable. They worshipped other gods, they perverted justice, and they straight up ignored God's Word.

So Jeremiah was called into ministry by God to prophecy to others of the destruction that was about to come to the city of Jerusalem. In fact, the whole beginning of the book was God's instruction to Jeremiah to prepare the people for God's coming destruction of Jerusalem. Because Jeremiah had a heart in tune with God's voice, he did just that; he warned the people that if they did not change their ways, then the Babylonians would destroy their city, and they would be exiled. Our God is a good and patient God, but we must never forget that He always keeps His promises. And God had promised to exile His people if they turned away from Him.

Along with Jeremiah's ministry, King Josiah (who was the king of Judah when Jeremiah began his ministry) also wanted to lead his people back to God. So a few years after Jeremiah began his prophetic work, a law book was discovered at the Holy Temple in Jerusalem. This law book is referred to in the Bible as the book of Deuteronomy (the Book of Law). This book was then made a part of the law of the land by King Josiah, who hoped to create change in people's hearts, correct social injustices, and protect the worship of God from outside influences. It was hoped that enforcing these laws

(God's laws written by Moses) would create the change the people so desperately needed in order to bring unity to their land.

Jeremiah was able to observe what it was like before and after these laws were introduced, and what he concluded was this:

There was no change.

I have to give King Josiah credit; his intentions were good. He wanted people to turn to God. Jeremiah wanted the same thing. However, it wasn't God's law that was the reason these reformation efforts failed, but rather it was the motives, inner attitudes, and condition of people's hearts. Jeremiah saw that people couldn't change their evil ways until they experienced a change of heart. Jeremiah, myself, and many of us know we can't change our human nature by ourselves. We can't change our nature, and we can't change the world through new leadership, new policies, or new laws.

We need Jesus.

The change they needed back then and the change we need now can only occur through a relationship with God, and God can only have the access to change our hearts when we turn to Him, recognize the need for it, and want to receive it. Without this inner transformation, all efforts to create change, peace, and unity are destined to fail. A solution without Jesus is like doing a jigsaw puzzle with some missing puzzle pieces. The puzzle is never going to be complete; we can't see the whole picture unless we have all the pieces.

If we read the Old Testament books in the Bible, we can see that this is the exact lesson the people of Israel learned thousands of years ago. We can also see what happens when people bring their real pain, sorrow, and repentance to God. The theme of many other books, especially in the Old Testament, is about bringing everything to God and realizing He truly is the solution to restoration in our hearts and in our lives.

But too often, what we see now is that too many people want to make our world whole again by attempting to build a bridge of peace and unity, and it is heartfelt and with the utmost good intentions and through grassroots efforts. However, they're trying to bring the wrong type of unity.

I know what you're thinking. How in the world is there a wrong type of unity? How can any version of unity be wrong? You have every reason to feel that way and ask those questions.

Allow me to elaborate.

Pastor Aaron Kennedy, at Open Door Church in North Carolina, spoke on the biblical concept of unity during one of his virtual sermons; he said one of his mentors taught him that there are two different types of unity: a "spirit of unity," and "unity of the Spirit."

There is a huge difference.

He explained it like this: The biggest difference between the two is that a spirit of unity creates sameness. Ultimately, the driving force behind a spirit of unity involves choosing a side—siding with people who are like-minded, people who think the same way you do, people who vote the same way you do, people who believe the same way you do. Churches are just as guilty. Religion even creates division. In the Bible, it was Jews and Gentiles—the origin of division.

I'm not saying it's a bad thing to stand for what you believe in; you should stand up for those who are oppressed and hurting. It's an admirable thing to contend for justice, but to do so without the unifying principles of Jesus Christ is like not having all of your puzzle pieces. And if you take a step back, what we're seeing right now is that the spirit of unity for the social, cultural, and political reformation efforts we're seeing in this world is actually creating more division among people. Remember that the enemy's main motive is disunity.

Pastor Aaron said that on the flip side, unity of the Spirit creates oneness. And whenever the Bible talks about unity, it specifically talks about unity in Christ only and through one Spirit. If you want to read about how the Bible instructs us to contend for unity, I strongly encourage you to read the book of Ephesians. Paul wrote this letter to the city of Ephesus, in an attempt to unify the Jews and

Gentiles. They were having the same problems back then that we are facing now. His instructions are no different for us today and are very clear on how we should be contending for unity: "Therefore I, the prisoner in the Lord, urge you to walk worthy of the calling you have received, with all humility and gentleness, with patience, bearing with one another in love, making every effort to keep the unity of the Spirit through the bond of peace" (Ephesians 4:1–3).

Not only are we talking about unity here, but the book of Ephesians also talks about the power that believers have, because the Holy Spirit lives inside of us. You see, culture is not capable of transforming a person or this world. Culture uses conformity and coercion to bring together people with the same thoughts and ideas as a way to contend for unity. Just as Jeremiah and King Josiah learned thousands of years ago, true and lasting change cannot occur through law, policy, and force. That is ultimately why Jesus came to die for our sins. We weren't capable of changing our sinful nature by ourselves; we simply were not strong enough to do it. The only One capable of transforming us is Jesus. He transforms with the power of His grace and love, which can only be done through a relationship with Him and a change of heart. It's the willingness of people to obey the unenforceable obligations. The gap that needs filling between our problems and our solution is Jesus. Believers are called to fill that gap, which is why living in the tensions of this world is exactly where we need to be. If we want to bring unity in the way God wants us to unify, then we just have to agree on one truth: that Jesus is the way, the truth, and the life. If we can agree on just that one, simple truth, then we can handle every single worldly difference with love, forgiveness, compassion, and prayer for one another.

Jesus's last moments before being crucified were spent in prayer. Jesus prayed for Himself, He prayed for His disciples, and He prayed for all believers—you and me. Jesus prayed for unity of the Spirit (italicized words are added for emphasis):

> I pray not only for these [His disciples], but also for those who believe in me through their word. *May they all be one, as you, Father, are in me and I am in you.* May they also be in us, so that the world may believe you sent me. I have given them the glory you have given me, so that they may be one as we are one. *I am in them and you are in me, so that they may be made completely one, that the world may know you have sent me and have loved them as you have loved me.* (John 17:20–23)

Through our relationship with God, we are able to look at the problems in this world through a lens that allows us to make sense of the tension going on around us and understand that the role we must play is to bring the type of unity that only comes through the Holy Spirit that we have through Jesus Christ.

There is no bigger agenda to advance than the Kingdom of God. God already wrote how everything is going to play out. The only thing we need to worry about is how to stand in the middle of the tension and direct hearts to move in the direction toward Jesus. The world so desperately needs people who have cultivated their hearts to the tenderness and bold truths about who Jesus is. The world needs people who know Jesus's heart. The world needs heavenly solutions to our earthly problems, and you and I play such an important role in that.

My brothers and sisters, let this be your encouragement. It's a tough, harsh world, but you and I were made for such a time as this.

CHAPTER 13
BE THE LIGHT AND THROW SALT

Jesus said Himself, "I have come as light into the world, so that everyone who believes in me would not remain in darkness." (John 12:46)

Jesus came to this world so believers in Him could bear witness to His light. The good versus evil in this world is synonymous with light versus darkness. During Jesus's Sermon on the Mount, He gave His disciples very direct instructions regarding Kingdom discipleship. Jesus was preparing them for their mission—the same mission that each and every one of us are called to today. His teachings emphasized the spiritual conduct that all believers must have if we are to be good stewards of God's truth and our revolutionary assignment to bring light into a very dark world. The type of mission He was preparing them for would be exemplified in Paul's teachings through his encouragement to the churches in Ephesus, as I discussed in the last chapter, when he wrote his letter to attempt to bring unity between the Jews and Gentiles.

Paul tells us to not be wrapped up in arguments and disobedience, because we must always remember that we believers were also once in the darkness. We had to be acquainted with the darkness in order for us to be able to appreciate the need for being in relationship with our source of light—Jesus. Let us never forget where we came from. Once we accepted Jesus Christ in our lives, we were born again into the light; as Paul said, "For you were once in darkness, but now you are light in the Lord" (Ephesians 5:8).

God gives us the power and strength to be the light in this world because it is through Him that we've been saved. That is the secret to reaching hearts and understanding where our power lies. This power allows you to be confident in what God is calling you to do. When you open your heart and allow God to align your life with His purpose and will, there is an undeniable light that shines within you, a light that has the power to pour onto others. This is why I've said that we must learn to love God first, before we can truly learn to love one another the way He wants us to. Discipline and alignment must come before the mission, and they must be continuously checked as we walk with Christ.

Following Christ is the hardest but most fulfilling thing we will ever do. It is a lifelong process of sanctification, which is why surrender must be a daily choice. The reason this is such a big challenge is because we must learn how to live in this world without being conformed to it; living your life God's way, doing His works to bring Him glory. It is a constant pursuit to seek godly discernment and balance in being the right amount of truth, seasoned with the right amount of grace. God is calling us to be bold enough to share His truths and gentle enough to extend His grace. As followers of Christ, we are not supposed to blend in; we are meant to stand out. We are meant to look, act, think, and speak differently than the rest of the world. We have been set apart to accomplish a very heavenly mission.

You see, salvation is so much more than forgiveness of our sins. We are called to be different because our salvation and the freedom we have in Christ allow us to break the chains and remove the shackles from the cultural straitjacket many people are in. The problem is, we don't dare to be different because culture and society have conditioned us to follow to the patterns of the world, or fit into a box, by making these conditions our standard for normalcy or popularity. The Bible calls it conformity. God's standards for righteousness go against everything this world stands for. We can dare to be different only when our identity is not tied to worldly validation and the need to please others before God. When you make the decision to follow Jesus, you're actually going against culture. You're even going against your own flesh. You will stand out and, unfortunately, will be misunderstood by many others. People won't understand the calling God has put on your heart. That's how we become the light; that's how we share our light. The light we share and the salt we throw is how we stand out, what makes us different. We *must* dare to be different.

The desire to follow Jesus must override the desire to be accepted by others. Believers are meant to walk outside their comfort zone because that's exactly how God uses us. Living outside our comfort zone requires us to depend completely on Him and not our own understanding of things. Simultaneously, it deepens our roots in our relationship with God. This walk is how God gently directs us to submitting to Him, answering our calling and stepping into our purpose. Let me remind you again that a submitted believer is the enemy's biggest threat.

How are we supposed to act, though? How do we know who God wants us to be?

Simply by spending time with Him. We must be students before we can be teachers. We learn who God wants us to be through seeking Him and allowing our hearts to be transformed through renewing our minds on a daily basis to His Word. This transformation allows the soil of our hearts to become more fertile so God can plant His seeds of truth; then we are able to truly discover and walk in our purpose, according to His will. We must choose Him daily, and faith must be our first instinct if we want to be all that God has called us to be. The quickest way to starve your faith is by indulging in your emotions and avoiding spending time with God.

I have to brush my teeth every day. Why? Because if I don't, my teeth are going to rot. The same goes for the Word of God. We must make time to be in God's presence and feed our faith with His Word, because if we don't, our faith will rot. Feeding our faith with the Word of God is like watering flowers so they can bloom. This is why His Word is referred to as "the bread of life." It's our soul food—literally. We are truly strengthened through rest and relationship. Without relationship, there is no rest. There is only constant striving and pursuit of short-lived gratification that only the world can give.

Jesus tells us that when we rest in Him, we find our strength. It is one of the most wonderful benefits of a relationship with Him. Continued rest, followed with continued strength, helps develop your confidence in Him. That confidence is what allows us to follow Jesus boldly and courageously, because our trust comes from His promises. This is needed in order to fulfill our duties in Jesus's teaching regarding discipleship on being the salt and the light of this world.

Jesus put some serious heavenly truth behind His declarations to His disciples.

You Are the Salt of the Earth (Matthew 5:13)

Many people are familiar with the infamous "salt and light" parable Jesus spoke of during His Sermon on the Mount. Jesus used these metaphors to explain what our spiritual conduct must look like in a world full of darkness and disbelief. Both are used to convey the message that the way we impact the world is through our identity and influence. In other words, and in the context of this book, we learn our identity through the alignment of God's presence and will in our lives, and we influence the world through the manifestation and works of the Holy Spirit in our hearts. Our influence is made possible by allowing God to work through us. When Jesus said, "You are the salt of the earth," He was talking about you.

We know that Jesus was full of truth and grace, always. If we are to act and speak with the same truth and grace, it first requires us to understand that as we speak truth to others, we must discern whether our words bring life, reflecting the character of our Savior, or bring condemnation and confuse the character of our Savior to others. As we plant seeds of truth and share the Gospel, our job is to do so in a way that sparks curiosity and creates a thirst for the Word of God. We want to speak and act in a way that makes others desire to know where our joy, hope, peace, and strength come from.

We are the salt, the seasoning of truth.

Everyone loves a little salt on their food; it adds flavor. But make sure you have a tall glass of water, because by nature, salty food makes you thirsty. That is how believers are meant to represent Christ. We add flavor to the Word of God. We want to carry ourselves in a way that make people thirst for more. His Word really is that good.

I'm sure I'm not the only one, but there have been times where I accidentally added too much salt to my food, and it became too salty to eat. Too much salt will ruin the taste of our food. This is why the constant pursuit of godly discernment is so important, because sometimes, too much truth, deplete of God's grace, can ruin people's attitudes toward Jesus. Truth without grace is harsh. We must never compromise God's truth, but we must also remember that our words should always be spoken in love. A relationship with Jesus is the only way to gauge our thoughts and control our words, in order to make sure they are in alignment with Jesus's character and truth of the Gospel. This doesn't mean everyone is going to accept you or interpret your words correctly, but it does mean that your words will be spoken from a heart of conviction, rather than a heart of condemnation. It is a delicate balance but absolutely necessary to building the type of influence God desires for us to have in this world. His desire for us to look to Him for discernment is how He disciplines us to glorify Him through our actions and words.

Other times, food isn't salty enough; it doesn't taste good because there's no flavor. It's bland and doesn't make us thirsty for more. If my food has no flavor, then it won't satisfy me. I probably won't eat it, and I definitely won't be asking for seconds. I definitely won't be asking who the chef is. If we are the salt, but we aren't using it to season our work, point people to God, and share His truth and the good news of the Gospel, then we aren't being spiritually productive for the Kingdom. "It's no longer good for anything but to be thrown out and trampled under people's feet" (Matthew 5:13).

Just as too much truth deplete of grace is harsh, grace without truth is useless. But here's the thing: Truth and grace, when used together, are influence. To be the salt of this world means to be the right amount of both truth and grace, just as Jesus was. Jesus came here to show us how it's done, which is why we look to Him for discernment. While the Jewish lawmakers and priests wanted their Messiah to bring hard-handed justice, Jesus had a different mission. His mission was to set people free, bind the broken-hearted, heal the hurting, and rescue us from sin. He fulfilled Old Testament prophecy to prove to us that He is the only way to heaven, and if we want to answer our calling and lead others to Him, we must learn how to throw salt, how to make people thirsty for Him.

You may read this and think it's too much work, or it's impossible. Let me give you some good news: When pursuing Jesus is your daily choice, and surrender becomes your lifestyle, what you'll find is that His will becomes your will. You develop a heavenly desire to reach hearts because that's what God desires. You want what God wants. You'll look to Him first in everything you do and say because you remember how His truth and grace convicted and saved you. That, my friends, is the moment you realize you are truly walking in your purpose, and from that comes the greatest joy you will ever experience. His Holy Spirit works within our hearts to give us a permanent disposition in recognizing the role we must play in the Kingdom. The greater our desire is to please Him, the greater our influence will be in this world.

As believers, we can't lose our flavor. Our seasoning is meant to bless those around us through our words and our actions. Paul said, "Let your speech always be gracious, seasoned with salt, so that you may know how you should answer each person" (Colossians 4:6).

You Are the Light of the World (Matthew 5:14)

Every time the power of the Holy Spirit is mentioned in scripture, it's related to sharing one's testimony and God's truth so that He will be glorified. He dwells in every believer so we can do what we're called to do: be ambassadors of light in this world, introducing people to His truth, love, and grace. Our light allows God to change lives and transform hearts. We glorify Him in all of our joy and even through our trials, because by doing so, people are witnessing the power of how He has moved, and how He continues to move, in our lives. God uses your story to paint a bigger picture of what He, and only He, is capable of. By allowing Him to live in you and through you, that is how we shine our light in this world.

> In the same way, let your light shine before others,
> so that they may see your good works and give glory
> to your Father in heaven. (Matthew 5:16)

God uses our light to help others navigate through the darkness in this world. Remember, our light is our influence. You don't need a microphone, fame, or a large social media following as a platform to shine your light. God wants to use you right where you're at. There are people around you He may be using you to reach.

Jesus chose a murderer, a prostitute, a tax collector, and a bunch of fishermen to shine their light and spread the Gospel to the ends of the earth. They didn't believe God could use them until they experienced the transformation that came with the acceptance of their new identity in Christ.

> Therefore, if anyone is in Christ, he is a new creation; the old has passed away, and see, the new has come! (2 Corinthians 5:17)

I think many people don't believe God can use them because they have a sinful past. We are ashamed of the things we have done. We know we're not perfect. If you want God to use you, you must leave the old version of yourself behind. We tend to always remember the bad decisions we made in the past, but we must also remind ourselves that we no longer live there. We no longer live in darkness, and we're not going back to visit. God doesn't hold it against us, so why should we?

As we learn to follow Christ courageously, the end result is never perfection. That's not possible. The reality of being a true follower of Christ is the complete opposite of perfection. Followers of Christ are really just a big bag of broken pieces, held together by a perfect, merciful Savior. It's the safest, most reassuring place to be. We should always remind ourselves that God still loved us and pursued us through our past mistakes, and He will love us through our future mistakes. He came alongside us, who were broken, just like His disciples, so we could show the rest of the world how God fixes broken people so He can use them. Our brokenness never disqualifies us from being used by God and in His Kingdom work. His grace humbles us, which allows us to give glory where glory is due. It's all because of Him. Jesus says we are the light of this world, but it is always His light that shines through us. We are the vessel in not only His workmanship, but through being examples of His character. God desires for us to constantly pursue Him, so we are taught how to fully and completely embody His grace and capacity to love, and to be extensions of that same grace and love to others.

Can you imagine if we all made it our priority to be examples of our God-given light in this world?

I can.

Picture this: You are in a massive stadium filled with tens of thousands of people. All of the lights are turned off. It's pitch black—total darkness—and everyone in the stadium is holding unlit candles. Then, one person lights a candle. Just one. Although that one candle is surrounded by darkness, you can still see that tiny light in the stadium, no matter where you are standing. The person holding that candle decides to share their light and use it to light the candle of the person next to them.

Now there are two tiny lights.

Both of those people decide to light the candle of the person next to them.

Now there are four tiny lights.

Eventually, so many candles are lit that the stadium is no longer dark anymore. The stadium is now full of so much light that everyone is able to see. If we all chose to shine our light and pour our light onto others, this world would be so bright that no one would walk in darkness. Even those who have not yet lit their own candle would be able to see.

Now, imagine if the stadium lights were on, and one person decided to light a candle. That light would be shining, but it wouldn't be as noticeable since all the lights are on. Our light shines brightest in darkness. Now, more than ever, is the time for God's children to shine.

Your light has the potential to start a fire. You have no idea how one single act of obedience could spark a move of God. I'm asking you to remember this the next time you think that one person is incapable of changing the world. Our world has been so damaged by darkness that it can feel like our efforts are insignificant. But the world doesn't change by one massive, solitary movement; it changes by inspiring minds and hearts, one at a time, lighting one candle at a time. There is nothing more powerful than having the Holy Spirit dwelling inside of you. That is your light; that is your fire. There is nothing more capable of overcoming darkness than believers who know their identity and desire to pursue their mission for the

Kingdom, to share their light with the world. There is no amount of darkness that can ever overcome your candle, your light. Share your light by sharing your story, along with the gift of grace that has freely been given to us from the One Who gives us our power, our light.

This chapter (or this book) may help light someone else's candle. Maybe this will encourage you to shine your light on someone you know, who might be struggling in the darkness. Maybe sharing a little love and light today could start a fire in someone's heart for Jesus. We won't always know the fruit of the seeds we plant, but if it's possible to change one heart and help another person find her or his light, it's totally worth the effort to sow the seeds.

What I do know is this:

God does not let any of our good works go to waste. He is a God Who has a track record of getting maximum usefulness out of the most broken people and seemingly insignificant circumstances.

We are called. It should be our mission to share our God-given light with the world, because Jesus gave His own life to save it.

Balance

Many times, I find myself discussing two very distinct realities, and I simultaneously find myself stuck, trying to be the balance of truth and grace that Jesus calls us to be. If you see me in person or follow me on social media, you will find me talking about one of two things: the coming judgment on this world, including the warning signs of the tribulation period, and the saving grace of Christ and the goodness of God.

As a follower of Christ, we aren't supposed to sugarcoat anything, and at the same time, we are also instructed not to compromise His Word. There is a heavenly balance that must occupy our mindset. So, I'm constantly asking God, "Is this going to push people away, or is this going to be the salt someone needs to make people thirsty for You?" Before I post anything to social media or share on my podcast, or before I wrote anything in this book, I make sure each and every word and thought comes with clarity and confirmation from God. Scripture says be slow to speak, and if my words don't align with the promptings and teachings of the Holy Spirit, I will wait, pray, and work on them until they do.

Being a follower of Christ is the hardest yet most joyful thing we will ever do. It is a privilege to follow Him, and with that anointing comes a Kingdom we must represent by picking up our cross and following Him daily. Following Christ will have you laying some uneasy truths on the hearts of others. These same truths may come with opposition, ridicule, and persecution. When people are confronted with God's truth, they will be either convicted or offended. Please be sure to love them, no matter what. But too many people these days do not want to face the opposition that comes with speaking about God's truths; they would rather accommodate others and be passive to the reality of the coming judgment and wrath of God this world will face one day.

It's 2021 as I write this book, and I'm looking at the condition this world is in and the direction it is moving, and I see an entire world that is being deceived and hearts becoming so hardened. I see people, Christians even, divided on so many issues. This world is moving in a very dangerous direction, and the Word of God, the founding principles of the United States, are being removed and pushed to the back burner of society. We have come to a place and time where people are no longer able to receive God's truth. Collectively, we don't fear God's truth or heed His warnings anymore.

We are living in an era of "my truth versus your truth." Society has allowed people to perceive whatever they want as truth. Your truth is based on what you believe to be true, what you feel is true. It is a problem, individually and as a nation, when our emotions and feelings dictate the truth we stand for. Not enough people see that what we are doing is leading future generations away from God. If you want to believe that a poisonous dart frog is your god, then by all means that is your decision. But it becomes a big problem if we become passive in accommodating these perceptions of truth as the standards for society.

REST IN THE RAINBOW

The best part about God's Word is that it is objective, and because of this, we have something we can use to base our moral values on. We know God's Word is true because His promises have never failed. His prophets were accurate and correct in their predictions, defying all odds of statistics. The definition of *objective* is "judgment that is not influenced by personal feelings or opinions in considering and representing facts."

The opposite of objectivity is subjectivity. The definition of *subjective* is "based on or influenced by personal feelings, tastes, or opinions." If our truth is based on subjectiveness, then we will never see unity; we will only see more division.

Even "being a good person" is subjective. Adolf Hitler thought his actions were leading to the making of a better world, although he had the blood of 6 million Jewish people on his hands. Muhammad, who claimed to be a prophet from Allah, ordered mass murder and assassinations, and is arguably the father of hostility between Muslims and Jews.

That is what those two individuals chose as the "righteous and just" thing to do, so because they thought they were being a good person and doing what was right, then they must be correct in their actions, right?

I'm sure you answered no to that question.

Is it because it's not socially acceptable to murder people? Says who?

But if they believe they are a good person, then they must be a good person, if that's what they believe, right?

Do you see the issue that subjectivity causes in this world?

See, we base morality and values on things that are socially acceptable, which is also subjective. Because what is socially acceptable is based on opinion, no matter which way you look at it or what side you stand on. And what I'm seeing today is that without God, everything in this world is subjective, based on someone's own personal opinion about what's right or good. Without God, how do we determine what is good or not? How do we determine what is right or not? And I'm going to be honest and say that morality, values, and "right and wrong" are being watered down, even by Christians themselves. Too many people are afraid to stand up for God because what God says and what His standards are go against the direction of this world. Entirely. God's standards are good. They are the way to righteous living. His standards are our instructions to how we should be living our lives.

But before you think I'm condemning anyone, let me say this: God knows we can't meet His standards. We don't have the power to do it. Our flesh is weak; we will always fall short. Every single one of us. There's absolutely nothing we can do to be righteous enough, to be a good enough person to be in the presence of the Holy, Holiest of Holy God. Since the beginning of time, humanity has been infected with sin.

I am thankful I have God's objective truth to live by. God's truth is how I dictate my life, and it is a good thing I don't have to make decisions based on my emotions. When we are being led by God, then we are being led by His objective standards. If we are not being led by God, then our choices are dictated by our emotions and how we feel. My point is, if we rely on the world or society to tell us what's good or right, then we are always going to be confused, we are always going to be influenced by others' opinions, we are always going to change our minds, and to be honest, we will live an exhausting life. There's never going to be one right way to believe, according to the world's standards. That's why we have God's standards; even though it is impossible to meet them, we have faith that Jesus met them for us. We are declared righteous by our faith, not by our own works or perceived version of being a good person. It's not up to us to decide what's good or right, because God decided that for us when Jesus came here to be our good news and our deliverance.

Which leads me to my next point.

One of the reasons God's truth has never been widely accepted is because we tiptoe around His wrath and judgment. To keep the truth very simple, if God dealt with us the way we deserved to be, no one would be able to stand before Him. No one would be worthy enough to be in His presence. There is going to come a time where those who have not placed their faith in Jesus Christ will be judged and sent to an eternity in hell. We talk about God's judgment because those who have placed their faith in Him have been spared of judgment. We talked about this in part 1. So while the truth of the Gospel is about peace, love, mercy, comfort, and strength, it is also about God's wrath, His judgment, and the coming tribulation period in this world that so many people are not prepared for.

We can't talk about God's love, without talking about His wrath.

We can't talk about God's grace, without talking about His standards.

We can't talk about God's forgiveness, without talking about His judgment.

The reason His followers serve and glorify Him is because the God's honest truth is that we don't deserve His love; we deserve His wrath. Humanity has always rebelled against God. He gives us forgiveness when we don't deserve it. The grace He gave us came at a heavenly cost. The reason we should talk about His wrath and judgment is because Jesus rescued us from it all.

We are people who might do good deeds, but works do not save us; faith does. The subjectivity of this world might say that I am a good person through the lens of society. But I'm here to tell you that I am not a good person; I am a saved person.

It is important to understand the current state of this world as part of our mission as followers of Christ, because while we are instructed to be the light of this world, we must also understand that our light isn't going to be understood by everyone. When you shine your light in this world, you're not only glorifying God and talking about His grace; you are also exposing the darkness and evil going on in society. When evil is brought to light, it stirs the enemy up. It's like shining a light in a dark room and watching the cockroaches scatter. Our light makes the enemy uncomfortable. Darkness has to move when light enters a room.

When Satan was kicked out of heaven and introduced sin to the world, he did everything he could to keep prophecy from being fulfilled. The Messiah was coming. The light was coming. The Savior was coming. You can see it played out in scripture how the devil did everything in his power to keep Christ from coming into this world. The devil saw the lineage that was going to give birth to the promised Messiah, which was why Esau was motivated by the devil to kill Jacob (who would be the father to Israel's twelve tribes); that's why he worked his evil ways in King Herod's heart to slaughter all of the Hebrew baby boys in Bethlehem; that's why the devil thought he won on the day Jesus was crucified. Little did he know, that event was our ultimate victory.

God thwarted all the enemy's plans, and because he couldn't stop God's plans, now he is trying to keep the world from a relationship with Christ. This is why the world must know God's truth. This is why we must no longer be passive in God's Word and the calling He has put on our heart. God wants to use us to shine His light and glorify His name through us.

We see in scripture that as God draws people into His presence, and even today, these people become a voice to their generation. Maybe you are feeling as if God is drawing you closer to Him right now. As you step closer and closer into your calling, and walk closer and closer with God, your identity is going to be attacked. As we get to the end of the book, I want to take a moment to talk once more about your identity as a child of God.

If you are being drawn into the presence of God, you are going to begin to feel unworthy and incapable. If this is happening to you, you might feel as if you are coming unfastened; by that I mean, you are becoming more and more aware of your deficiencies, your weaknesses, your shortcomings. You are becoming more aware of the issues in your character you might not have noticed before you began a relationship with Christ. You become aware of your unholiness and unworthiness. This has always been the pattern and process of the prophets and disciples throughout scripture. As Moses, Isaiah, Jeremiah, Daniel, Paul, John, and others stepped into their relationship with God and were filled with the Holy Spirit, they became aware of their shortcomings and unholiness. At the same time, when they were in the presence of God, they became aware of His perfect holiness and righteousness. Because they were aware of this, they were also able to learn who they truly were without God.

If you are currently feeling this way, or if you haven't stepped into a relationship with God, just know that if you want Him to use you in a significant way, then you must go through this process. You must allow God's truth and presence to expose the areas of your life that don't serve Him. So if you feel that your identity is being attacked, or the feelings of unworthiness begin to consume you, my advice to you is this:

Don't let the devil condemn you before you allow God to show you who you are and what you can do because of Him.

God has to show us who we really are without Him; that way, when He does the things in our lives that only He can do, He will get all the glory. We get none of it. That is how He uses us. That is why our light is so important.

Proud people can't represent Christ. He must get all the credit and glory because that is how we testify to others. What God does through our lives becomes our message to the fallen masses in this world.

Our light is not only about speaking truth to people; it is also about the bold and audacious faith to believe that God wants to use you in ways that glorify Him and show the world around you exactly what faith and relationship look like with Him. Even if people don't want to listen to what you say about the Word of God, they will see and witness Christ living in you, doing things that only God can do. This is why we don't take any credit for what God does through us, because remember, we represent the Kingdom. When you take credit, as a follower of Christ, you give a false sense to the world around you that the things you accomplished are through your own power and strength.

We see too many people taking the credit and glory for God's works these days. This probably plays a role in why a lot of people feel they don't need God. There is nothing good or godly about the word *pride*.

This is why we are also allowed to believe in God for things that are outside our means or resources. When you step into your purpose, God will prompt you to do a lot of things that are outside your means. That's why He requires complete dependence and surrender. If you want God to use you in mighty ways, you need to have a mighty faith. Allowing God to work through you will cause even devout atheists to look at your life, see your obedience and your faith, and say to themselves, "There has to be something bigger and powerful that is leading this person in their life. There is something about this person that is different from the rest of this world."

My friends, don't underestimate the power of your light.

God's children, the light of this world, are the only examples of truth and grace we have left.

CHAPTER 14
UNWRAPPING YOUR GIFT

God is the ultimate gift-giver; He loves to give. In fact, He gave His only Son as a gift to this world, so that those who believed in Him could receive even more gifts as a benefit of a relationship with Him. We've talked about the gift of salvation and the gift of grace abundantly throughout this book. Let me give you a couple of promises as a refresher:

The gift of salvation: "For the wages of sin is death, but the gift of God is eternal life in Christ Jesus our Lord" (Romans 6:23).

The gift of grace: "For you are saved by grace through faith, and this is not from yourselves; it is God's gift—not from works, so that no one can boast" (Ephesians 2:8–9).

Yet there is one gift that I haven't quite touched on, and it's an integral part of our growth, calling, and mission. In order to fulfill our mission, in order to execute His assignment, we must first understand that the way He fulfills this is through our individual spiritual gifts.

Our gifts allow for the Holy Spirit to be evidenced through our lives; your gifts are empowered by the Holy Spirit. God designs us with different and unique gifts that allow Him to advance us in our calling, motivate others, and improve the lives of those around us. Our gifts create impact and influence because as we practice them and step into them, God ministers through us. Walking in our purpose becomes easier and more effective when we are actively using our God-given, spiritually instilled gifts.

I wish you could fill out a checklist to determine what your unique spiritual gift is. But I hope you understand by now that the purpose of developing a relationship with God and surrendering to Him is so He can reveal these things to you as you walk with Him. Only God can reveal to you what your unique gifts are. Whether you believe it or not, God has been walking with you and preparing you your whole life for the moment you step into your purpose. Discovering your gift is like finding your sweet-spot with God; it provides an intimate level of clarity that takes your relationship with God to a whole other level. Knowing what your gifts are allows you to get in your spiritual groove for the part you have to play in the Kingdom work—the mission. Just as God gave gifts to us, we must give our gifts to others. This is not only how we grow; it's also how we lead others to Jesus. Stepping into our gifts and allowing God to shine through us helps us add the flavor of our Savior to the world and bring out the best in others.

My late grandfather, Randall, had a very special gift. He was blessed with the gift of gardening. My Papaw had an enormous garden, and fruit trees were planted all around his home. He believed that the purpose of harvesting so much fruit was so that he could give it away. And that's what he did. He worked hard to use his God-given gift to serve and feed people. I grew up on a farm, so as a kid, I always ran around barefoot. Not at Mamaw and Papaw's house, though, because if you did, there was a good chance you would twist your ankle on some fallen fruit scattered all over their backyard; that gives you an idea of how many fruit trees there were. Papaw loved Jesus, and His love for Him was displayed to others through his generosity. He grew fruits and vegetables just to give them all away. The fruit of the Holy Spirit was evidenced in his life, literally.

Gifts are not to be mistaken as talents; there is a big difference. Often times, our talents are often things we equate to our grind and performance. You can get better at anything you choose to focus your time and effort on. A professional basketball player doesn't become a first-round draft pick overnight. Talents are made more proficient through practicing them. Talents are also a way we form our identity. Many people strive to be known by their stats and accomplishments. However, God calls us to live a life of significance over success. A life of significance is not in what you accomplish, but in what you do for others, and let me tell you, leading others to God and helping save souls is the most significant thing you can do in this life. This is why understanding what your gifts are is so important, because your gift is something God gave you as He knitted you in your mother's womb.

Discovering your gift is a prerequisite to pursuing your purpose. God works in you by using your spiritual gifts to display His power so that it points to Him. This is what living a life of significance is all about. Our purpose involves using our gifts for Him, to lead others to Him. Once we discover our spiritual gifts, our purpose is to give them away. Our gifts help to give us clarity of our purpose in life.

Our talents will lead us to a successful life; our gifts are what lead us to a life of significance. Don't get me wrong; there's nothing wrong with having a successful life. But so many of us go through life accomplishing and acquiring so many material things, job titles, and letters behind our name, but we never feel truly fulfilled. We still find ourselves looking for purpose. The purpose we are looking for can only be fulfilled when we are living for God, not for the world.

If you need help finding where to start as you begin to search for your spiritual gift, ask yourself these questions:

What are you passionate about?

What are you good at? What do others say you're good at? What brings you joy?

What comes naturally to you?

The reason we are passionate about things is because God put them in our heart with the intention for us to develop that same passion into our gifts, which are meant for us to share with the world. You were born in God's eyes to serve His purpose, be a positive influence on others, and make disciples as you lead others to Him. God gave us these special gifts as leverage to be able to do so. The things you are most passionate about probably play a role in your calling.

However, in order to use your gift properly, and in the most fulfilling way, you must spend time asking God to help you understand where in your life He wants you to use it. This can only be understood through time and prayer. Your gift is special; no one can ever take it away from you. It is something God strategically and permanently placed in your heart.

> God's gracious gifts and calling are irrevocable.
> (Romans 11:29)

Only God can truly reveal and connect the answers you are searching for. Open your Bible, trust in Him, listen for His voice, and it will come to you in His perfect timing. When we desire to hear from Him and seek Him, just as He told the prophet Jeremiah:

> Call to me and I will answer you and tell you great
> and incomprehensible things you do not know.
> (Jeremiah 33:3)

Your gift is with you; you may just need to do a little more unwrapping.

Just as God made each one of us unique in appearance, we are also uniquely identified through our spiritual gifts. The apostle Paul had a lot to say about the diversity of spiritual gifts, as he recognized how important gifts are to building up the body of believers:

> Now concerning spiritual gifts: brothers and sisters, I do not want you to be unaware. ... Now there are different gifts, but the same Spirit. There are different ministries, but the same Lord. And there are different activities, but the same God produces each gift in each person. A manifestation of the Spirit is given to each person for the common good. (1 Corinthians 12:1, 4–7)

In other words, we all have different, yet equally important roles to play in God's Kingdom work, by using our gifts. This is why you see teachers, mentors, missionaries, cooks, writers, and musicians investing and stepping into their God-given gifts. The way we reach people may be different, but it's the same God, the same Spirit.

In order to unlock the potential of your gift that has already been given to you to be an influence in this world, you have to do several things:

You Must Chase after Spiritual Maturity

In order to fully apply your spiritual gifts, you need to mature in your relationship with God first. Pursuing God requires you to humble yourself before Him. God desires to broaden your thinking and deepen your insight. Maturing in a relationship with Him teaches you how to depend on Him for the wisdom, strength, and confidence you need in order to pursue your purpose. Just as an infant must start with milk, progress to soft food, and then move to solid food, God works the same way. Learning His way of thinking, the heavenly treasures of His Word, and the spiritual discernment needed to accomplish His will is a process that requires time and surrender. We must feed ourselves with the Word.

God knows what we need and will only reveal to us as much as we need in order to remain dependent on Him. That is how we develop an understanding of His Word. That is how we learn. Another thing we learn as we chase after spiritual maturity is that our gifts need practice and investment, too. I tried to write a book before this one, and it failed miserably. I believe the reason it failed was because although I believed writing was my gift and my passion, I wasn't using it as God's vessel; it wasn't going to glorify Him the way He is supposed to be glorified, and I wasn't using my gift to point people to Him. Although I had good intentions, I hadn't quite matured enough spiritually to understand that God wanted to use me in more fruitful ways for His Kingdom.

Before I wrote this book, and as I was going through my bowel reconstruction surgeries, I wrote blogs, telling my story of brokenness, God's redemption, and what His grace had done for me. I will never forget the revelation God gave me when I asked Him if it was in His plan for me to continue my blogs or begin writing this book. The Holy Spirit interrupted my thinking with a convicting heavenly whisper that said, "Your blogs were just practice for this."

Spiritual maturity is understanding what God has done in you to understand what He can do through you. When God reveals to you how He wants you to use your gifts in the world, there's absolutely no one who can tell you any different. His conviction always comes with confirmation.

The point is, we are all children of God. Not once in the Bible will you find human beings referred to as "God's adults." If we don't reach a level of humility and maturity first, we are going to live our lives like defiant teenagers, thinking we know what's best without seeking God's Word, clarity, and confirmation first. This is because we are constantly being disciplined, sanctified, and used to accomplish His will our whole lives. We must always be dependent on our heavenly Father. We must develop God's character and grow in spiritual maturity in order for our gifts to be fully explored and exhibited.

You Must Change the Way You See Yourself

Gifts + Voice = Power. Part of changing the way you see yourself involves understanding that you are far more powerful than you give yourself credit for. We've talked about our identity throughout this book, but I must remind you again, because we must always remember the permanent target we have on our back. The enemy wants you to keep your spiritual gifts in the closet. He wants your purpose to collect dust. He doesn't want God to use you, because the enemy knows that when He does, it exposes his weakness. He loses his power when you step into yours. The only power the enemy has is to tempt us or trick us out of the authority and power we have as children of God. We must constantly remind ourselves of who we are as children of God because as we discover and use our gifts, we will experience resistance. We will experience spiritual warfare. Those familiar thoughts of fear, doubt, and worry are going to knock on your prefrontal cortex (the part of your brain responsible for emotional control and judgment). We are all vulnerable to the flaming arrows of spiritual warfare; not one of us is immune. The way you see yourself has nothing to do with how you feel, and everything to do with what God says. You must get to a point where you continuously choose not to trust your emotions. Your emotions are deceitful and easily manipulated. God's Word and His promises never change. You can write them on your heart and keep them as ammunition.

You will need it.

However, once we see ourselves the way God sees us, we will begin to invest more and more in our relationship with Him and desire to know how He wants to use us. Nothing will bring you greater joy than doing what God calls you to do, leading a life of significance, and planting seeds of hope and truth.

There are people out here with an empty spiritual tank, directionless, unsure where the source is to discovering purpose. They have a gift inside of them that has never been unwrapped. Those same people need to know how God wants to work through

them. For that reason, they need to hear how God is working through you. They need to see how God is using your gifts to lead others to Him. And if you already have a relationship with God, then you have a Holy Spirit dwelling inside of you.
Tap. In.
You've got the fire; God's got the match. Invest in your passions, spend time exploring what makes you happy, and ask God to show you things that only He is capable of revealing. In a world full of darkness, we need to let God ignite that passion so we can be the light. Investing in our spiritual gifts, and using them, will help others find and use theirs. God has a good plan for everyone. He's waiting for us to tap in. When we change the way we see ourselves, we aren't afraid to shine.

You Must Get out of Your Comfort Zone (and Stay There)

God is calling you higher because you have a story to tell and people to reach. Our gifts allow us to live a purposeful life, and they also help unlock the potential in others and inspire them to live bigger, believe bigger. Our gifts enable us to live out our testimony, our story. The fifteen years of chronic illness was the preparation I needed from God to step into my calling and invest in my spiritually instilled gift: writing. God turns our pain into purpose, if we're willing to get out of our comfort zone and see it from His perspective. It wasn't until I embraced my gift of writing that I was able to find another level of joy and fulfillment. Working in your gift is how you draw people closer to God. It's always about Him, and that is exactly where God wants you. And what you find is that living outside your comfort zone is a fun and adventurous place to be when you trust God; it's taking leaps of faith daily and leaving the outcome up to God. Our desire to have control is not found outside our comfort zone either, because this is where God is able to deliver some of His biggest miracles. He loves doing impossible things. That's how He shows us that He is God.

Activating your gift is a part of your heavenly assignment (which we will talk about in the next chapter), because through activation, you are allowing God to use you as a vessel; this allows God to work and manifest Himself in the lives of those around you. Using your gift isn't always comfortable, convenient, or easy, but neither is obedience or surrender. We must learn why obedience and surrender are required in order to fully and courageously pursue our purpose. This is where our faith must be intentional and audacious. It's not about only trusting God in our current circumstances, but it's also about living expectantly. Living expectantly means believing God is calling you to elevate your purpose so that His presence can be evidenced through your life to others.

What you will see is that as you tap into your spiritual gifts, you will be able to experience the power of what God is doing in your life and the lives of others. The turning point in our relationship with God comes when we begin investing in our gifts. The product of this is where we begin to see the manifestation of the Holy Spirit's fruit in our lives and others'.

Activating and working in your gift is what running the race is all about. Our purpose is helping others find theirs. This is why we find ourselves out of our comfort zone a lot. Never once will you see in the Bible a story of God's miracles in someone's life who was living in their comfort zone. God is calling us higher. You and I are made for great things. God wants to do incredible and impossible things in your life and in the lives of the people you reach, but God needs you to trust Him, lean on Him, and listen to Him. He desires for you to do these things so He can work through you.

We are made in God's image, so we know He did not create us to be mediocre. Since that's the case, do you really think He would give us mediocre gifts?

CHAPTER 15
HEAVENLY ASSIGNMENT

The most hated people in history and in this world are Christians.

Eleven Christians are killed every day for their faith in Jesus Christ. In fact, one in eight believers worldwide experience high levels of persecution, just for following Jesus (Lowry 2019).

The Christian persecution we read about in the Bible is not just a thing of the past. Although the early Christians faced severe levels of martyrdom, Christians today are facing the same type of persecution.

As I'm writing this, I'm sitting in a public library, with a Bible open next to me. This would be a crime and cause for imprisonment or death in other countries. In North Korea (who is ranked first on the World Watch List for Christian persecution), this simple act would be a death sentence. In many Islamic states, such as Iran, Afghanistan, Somalia, and Pakistan (there are many others), becoming a Christian convert is considered an act of insanity; converts are vulnerable to arrest, violent abuse, rape, and murder.

Not only is this a call to action, for the prayer for our brothers and sisters in Christ who are persecuted and murdered for their faith in Jesus, but this should be the determining point that lifts the veil to some heavy, uncomfortable truths. It wouldn't be an act of love if I told you that following Christ was easy. The early disciples gave us some clear messages about persecution. John says, "Do not be surprised, brothers and sisters, if the world hates you" (1 John 3:13).

Jesus also put it like this: "If the world hates you, understand that it hated me before it hated you. If you were of the world, the world would love you as its own. However, because you are not of the world, but I have chosen you out of it, the world hates you" (John 15:18–19).

As a follower of Christ, you have been set apart to do work for God's Kingdom and to bring Him glory. The reason Christians, especially those being persecuted, are able to be courageous in their faith is because they know what God has promised them. They understand that Jesus told His disciples these things so His followers could have rest and take heart in carrying the victory of the cross on our hearts, even if that means dying for it. True rest and comfort can only come from the promises of God, and we know that Jesus has already conquered the world (John 16:33).

If it weren't for the courageous faith of Abraham, Moses, Daniel, Joshua, Paul, John, and so many others, chances are, we probably wouldn't have a Bible to read. There wouldn't be much of a story to tell of the miraculous power of God and the perfect track record of God keeping His promises. We wouldn't be able to read stories about breakthroughs. We wouldn't be able to comprehend the depth of God's love for us. Courageous faith means that our love for God must be greater than our love for worldly validation. Despite the relentless persecution the church has faced throughout the centuries, the church is still growing like never before. Revival is happening around the world. Souls are being saved in the name of Jesus.

And the Bible is still the number one best-selling book of all time.

I am deeply concerned that the American church is not ready to have their faith challenged, and I worry that we are not ready to face persecution the way many Christians in the Middle East are facing it as we speak. The United States is far from being on the Top 50 on the World Watch List of Christians facing extreme levels of persecution. Unfortunately, there will come an appointed time where people will be shaken out of their complacency, in the wake of the coming tribulation period, when God will pour out His judgment on those who have rejected Him.

That is one of the reasons for writing this book. My urgency to share the Gospel comes from two polar extremes: Every day, I'm full of both overwhelming joy and overwhelming sadness. My joy comes from what I have to look forward to in heaven. My joy is permanently rooted in my relationship with Jesus Christ and the incredible honor I have in serving Him. Yet my sadness comes from knowing that this world is so lost and there are still so many souls and hearts that need to find Jesus.

I feel the urgency and conviction to plant seeds for the purpose of helping others learn how to be bold in their faith; to help people, both believers and nonbelievers, understand that despite the lies the world may have told you, you have a very special assignment here on earth.

As followers of Christ, we are all called to the same mission, but each of us have different assignments. For the same reason our military has the same mission—to serve and protect—each person who serves in the military are called to different tasks and assignments. The mission we all have in the Kingdom army is to lead people to Christ and glorify our Lord. The assignment, however, is in our calling and how God directly uses us (and our gifts) as a vessel to reach the lost.

Your heavenly assignment is God-given. There is a dream or an idea God has planted in your heart, and He has equipped you with your spiritual gifts in order to work in your sweet spot with Him. Your assignment is not optional, although some believe it is. Our walk with God is not intended to be boring or complacent. God calls us to bigger and bolder things; He is capable of opening doors that no man can shut. Here's the thing: Your assignment is not for your benefit; it's for others. Your assignment is designed to influence others. That's why God intentionally designs us with our own spiritual gifts. Our gifts are to be used in a way to help lead others to Christ.

> Don't neglect the gift that is in you ... practice these things; be committed to them, so that your progress may be evident to all. Pay close attention to your life and your teaching; persevere in these things, for in doing this you will save both yourself and your hearers. (1 Timothy 4:14–16)

As you continue reading this last chapter, please take the time to reflect on the entirety of this book. I made this chapter the last one for a reason. Our assignment becomes evident once we begin maturing in our relationship with God, allowing Him to constantly sanctify and discipline us, and once we learn that, obedience and surrender become our lifestyle because we desire for God to properly use us.

God of the Ages

Too often, we forget that the God Who lives today is the same God Who parted the Red Sea. He is the same God Who dried up the water of the Jordan River for Joshua and the Israelites. He is the same God Who raised Lazarus from the dead. He is the same God Who brought healing through just the touch of Jesus's robe. He is the same God Who made the sun stand still for Joshua. Those miracles recorded in scripture aren't exceptions to what God can do. God desires to show up in miraculous ways because that's simply who He is. The earthly ministry of Jesus was defined by miracles. Part of having a Kingdom mindset is living in a permanent posture of miraculous expectations. God desires us to expect miracles. If we don't live with these expectations, we subconsciously put limitations on what God can do. We are allowed to believe bigger, because God is bigger than anything we could ever imagine. We too often forget who God really is.

God isn't someone you make time for. Your relationship with God should always be intentional. How often you spend time with God directly impacts your relationship with Him. When you truly walk with God, and when you obey His nudges and whispers, you become a witness to the fruit He is producing in you and others. You become a witness to how His miraculous grace truly transforms hearts. The reason people are so passionate about God, and the reason people are so unapologetically bold in their faith, is because they know the power of salvation. They know the authority that comes with being a child of the King. And when we walk in the power and authority of God, of the Holy Spirit in our lives, darkness breaks. Demons flee. The enemy loses his grip on God's children. Souls are saved.

We live to serve God. We live to worship God. The One Who gave us breath is worthy of every single bit of the glory.

He desires for us to have audacious faith, because that is how He is best glorified. I truly believe that trusting God for impossible things is how He takes our works and turns them into miracles. Our trust and dependence on God allow Him to work through us and accomplish things we would never be able to accomplish on our own.

When God calls you to something, it's because He is wanting to fulfill His ministry through you. You are the vessel. You are the boots-on-the-ground. You are His Kingdom ambassador. This is why part 1 of this book discussed learning to allow God to align His heart with yours. We have to be students before we can be teachers. Before we can walk in our purpose, we must understand how to be still in God's presence. He is with you everywhere you go.

The most in line you'll ever feel with your purpose in life is when your will aligns with God's will; when His will becomes your will. That is when you understand that your purpose is so much bigger than you thought, because it is rooted in heavenly places. That is when you are able to walk in confidence, knowing you are a unique expression of God, and He put you here to accomplish good works through you.

Just like the assignments of those in scripture, God desires for you to take your faith in Him to unspeakable heights, so He can work impossible miracles in your life and those around you.

We must believe that the God in scripture is the same God Who lives today. We have His rainbows to always remind us of this.

> For nothing will be impossible with God. (Luke 1:37)

Modern-Day Joshuas

Whenever I read the Bible, I like to put myself right in the pages of scripture. I try to imagine myself in their shoes, and when I do, the first thing that comes to mind is how much I admire the confidence and faith God's people had when carrying out their assignments.

After the death of Moses, Joshua became the new leader in Israel, and his assignment was to lead the Israelites into their God-promised land. The only problem was, there were already people living in this land, so these battles were not going to be easy conquests. Joshua had a very intimate relationship with God, and he was going to need God's guidance now more than ever, if he was going to lead a whole nation to victory.

As you read scripture leading up to this feat of Joshua's, you'll see that one of his first tasks was for him and his people to cross the Jordan River. God had to reassure Joshua four times before he crossed the Jordan. God reminded Joshua to "be strong and courageous." He also reminded Joshua several times that just as He was with Moses, He would be with Joshua too. It's my assumption that Joshua needed those words of encouragement, and God knew it. God knows we need courage, especially when we are stepping out in faith and acting out of our comfort zones in obedience to Him.

When we are on our God-given assignments, leaps of faith are going to have to be our primary mode of transportation. Dependence on God must be second nature to us. If we are called to walk boldly in our assignments, through acts of faith, we must stay close to God. God knows this. He knows that living a life committed to following Him is not going to be easy, and you are going to have to rest in His promises before you rest in your own understanding.

But just as He was with Moses, He is with us too, always.

> I will be with you, just as I was with Moses. I will not leave you or abandon you. (Joshua 1:5)

The only way we are able to find the courage and strength to live and walk as ambassadors for Christ is to continuously meditate on the Word of God. God's Word to us is this:

> This book of instruction must not depart from your mouth; you are to meditate on it day and night so that you may carefully observe everything written in it. For then you will prosper and succeed in whatever you do. (Joshua 1:8)

The more we understand God's ways, through studying His Word and being in His presence, the more equipped we are in making sure our heart is always in the right place and that we are living out our mission and assignment as He intends us to. As a result of this obedience, of pursuing God with an insatiable hunger and desire to please Him, we will witness more fruit of the Holy Spirit. That is the success we are promised.

You can see for yourself in chapter 10 in the book of Joshua what happens when our hearts are truly disciplined in God's Word. As Joshua and his soldiers are securing the victory of yet another battle, Joshua instructed them to put their feet on the necks of the five kings they were about to execute. Directly after, you can catch

Joshua saying to his soldiers, "Do not be afraid or discouraged. Be strong and courageous, for the Lord will do this to all the enemies you fight" (Joshua 10:25).

Do you see what happened here? The promise of God became so engraved in Joshua's heart that it also became his message to others. This is what God desires. God's truth is not only meant to comfort and strengthen us; His message and truths are meant to discipline us in such a loving way that once we understand the depth and nature of God's love and the authenticity of His promises, we are able to come alongside others in a way that points to Him. To be a modern-day Joshua is to walk in our heavenly assignments, in unwavering faith and confidence.

The way God works through His people (in their own free will, at that) is the most powerful demonstration this world will ever know.

Misfits Fit for the Kingdom

> Do not be conformed to this age, but be transformed by the renewing of your mind, so that you may discern what is the good, pleasing, and perfect will of God. (Romans 12:2)

In the beginning of this chapter, I talked about Christians being the most hated people in this world. Well, I'm sure this comes as no surprise to you that Christians are some of the most misunderstood people in this world, as well. The problem is, many Christians don't look different from the rest of the world. God calls us to have audacious, daring, bold faith, yet many Christians are walking around living spiritually unproductive lives. This isn't due to the fact that we deny God's existence, but we doubt His effectiveness.

The opposite problem is, these days, standing up for bold biblical truth will have you labeled as harsh, judgmental, or mean. Sadly, we only have ourselves to blame. We live in a world that is so sensitive to offense that we've sacrificed our confidence in the Gospel for a watered-down, lukewarm, compromised version of Christianity, all because we don't want to offend anyone, or we're afraid of what people might think of us.

So we've replaced conviction with offense, and that has made it easy for people to dismiss the Gospel and mock the power of our salvation as a joke or a fairy tale. This passive approach is dangerous. Being passive about truth is not love.

The truth is, I don't want the fluffy, feel-good, comfortable Christianity. And you shouldn't want that, either. I want the uncomfortable, inconvenient, convicting, good, powerful God Almighty Gospel because that is what heals us and that is what changes us. Living outside our comfort zone is exactly where God wants us, because that is where we learn to truly live in dependence on Him. That is how we walk boldly and unashamed. God shows us how to teach the minds and reach those who are spiritually blind.

If we truly love one another, why would we want anything less?

Understand this: Your assignment, and what God calls you to do, won't make sense to everyone, especially to those who have not yet learned how to walk in faith. Your answer to your calling will set you apart from others. You won't think the same as others; you won't look or act like the rest of the world. You walk in the authority of the King. Remember, you are not of this world, so you will be misunderstood; that is a guarantee.

We aren't supposed to fit in. A synonym for *misfit* is "nonconformist," and that's exactly what we are as children of God. It says in scripture that people were offended by Jesus. People hated Him for no reason, and He was murdered at the hands of those who did not understand Him. People hate what they don't understand. Your assignment will come with resistance and opposition. The closer you are to walking in your assignment and God's will, the harder the enemy is going to attack. Trust me.

This is why we should take heed to how our character must align with His truth and grace. I would argue that understanding the character of Jesus is the most important step to fulfilling our mission and carrying out our assignments. In every situation, we ask ourselves, "What would Jesus do? How would He respond?" Following Christ is the constant pursuit of seeking godly discernment.

Let me remind you once more that our mission is the same for all of us, but our assignments will look different. The mission of God's people is to make more disciples, but it's unlikely that I will have an assignment similar to Joshua's. It's unlikely that your assignment is the same as mine. But all of our assignments serve the same purpose: to lead others to God and to give God all the glory.

Don't forget that living for Christ is not about how famous you can get or how loud you are. It's about your influence. Your submission to God and His will for your life is the enemy's greatest threat. The Great Commission to "make disciples of all nations" is intended to have a ripple effect in this world. We lead people to Jesus by following Him, so others can learn how to do the same thing. That's how we build the Kingdom up; that's how we spread the good news of the Gospel.

The cancel culture movement of this generation is moving people further and further away from God's truth and His standards. The God-fearing truth of the Gospel goes against the mainstream attitudes of society, and the bolder you are for Christ, the more likely it is that you will be labeled as brainwashed or a conspiracy theorist. This world is in need of some misfits. The world needs God's troops who are unashamed and unapologetic of what it means to follow Christ. Following Christ is the most uncomfortable yet safest place we can be.

God is telling us today, "Get comfortable with being uncomfortable. Get comfortable with people not liking you. Get comfortable with people dismissing you because of Me. Get comfortable with speaking hard truths. Get comfortable with being 'too much' for those who don't want to listen."

And at the same time, God is telling us: "Get ready. Get ready for a new season of your life where you take the unashamed Gospel to a whole new level. Get ready for Me to open doors that you would never be able to open yourself. Get ready to watch Me set people free. Get ready to let Me use you to glorify My name. Get ready to watch Me move another mountain."

God has moved mountains before, and we will see Him do it again.

God-Sized Dreams

"By definition, a God-sized dream is beyond your ability, beyond your resources. If a dream is from God, it will require divine intervention" (Batterson, 195).

If your dream does not require divine intervention, then it's not big enough.

Assignments usually begin as a dream, a seed God has planted in your heart. With every miraculous encounter and fulfillment that you read about in scripture, there is one thing in common: the assignments that were given to God's faithful children all needed godly intervention. The odds were never in their favor. There was absolutely no way Moses could have parted that Red Sea by his own strength; if he did, then God wouldn't have received any of the glory. God did that to show His people that because of Moses's faith, God was able to show up in mighty, supernatural ways.

You better believe that as God calls you to your assignment, by planting dreams in your heart, and whispers in your prayers, He is going to prompt you to do things outside your means, resources, and networks. He will have you talking about some things that won't make sense to a lot of people. Faith is the willingness to look foolish. God-sized dreams require extraordinary faith. But that's how God moves in miraculous ways. You see, God never intended for us to just read about His miracles; He intended for us to be a part of them, as well.

If you are waiting for 100 percent clarity to move forward in your assignment, or if you're waiting for the right timing to pursue your God-given dream, then you will be waiting your entire life.

If you are waiting until you are ready, then you will never take the first step. If you feel stuck or stagnant in your relationship with God or your calling, then I urge you to spend more time in His Word. God's assignment will always come with clarity and conviction, not confusion.

It's also important to understand that while God is a God of clarity, your assignments will usually come with limited information. God isn't going to tell you everything you need to know because He desires us to depend on Him. However, He will always give you enough information needed to take the next step. In the book of Genesis, when Abram (before his name was changed to Abraham) was called to leave Haran, his home, God told him to "go out from your land, to the land that I will *show* you" (Genesis 12:1).

God never specifically said where he was taking Abram, nor did he give him a map. This is something to take note of when it comes to the things that God is calling us to do. Mankind has an intrinsic independent nature, which is why it is crucial to understand and embrace the nature of God first. We tend to avoid situations that make us feel uncomfortable. We tend to cringe at the unknowns.

Even Moses knows how you feel. He had a speech impediment, and when God told him to go Pharaoh in Egypt and demand he "let his people go," Moses begged God to send someone else. Begged.

My favorite part about the Bible is the fact that God deliberately chose imperfect people to carry out His assignments. Moses didn't feel qualified enough, but we can see throughout scripture that God uses the most unqualified people to accomplish His plans. The problem is, not enough of us have the bold and audacious faith to believe that He can do it. The difficulty in seeing our God-given dreams come true is our belief in Him that they will. It's not that we lack confidence in ourselves, it's that we lack confidence in God. The hardest part is not compromising our confidence in Him at the first sign of setback, doubt, or failure. When our intentions are pure and we are seeking God's direction, we must be able to embrace failure or disappointments as God's divine intercession and redirection.

We have to understand that faith in action requires God to move. Faith in action always results in an action of God. God always goes before us and is our protector behind us, but He can never take that step for us. We can stand in front of an open door all day, but we will never be able to experience the blessings and reward if we don't step through it.

Faith without works is dead. (James 2:26)

Have you heard of the phrase, "Don't just talk about it, be about it?" Well, the same goes for your God-given assignment; your prayer ethic must be consistent with your work ethic. It's also worth mentioning that if your end goal is fame and wealth, then allow me to love you enough to say that your heart is not in it for the right reasons. The only name we should desire to make famous is the name of Jesus. If fame and wealth become your blessings, then we must not forget that every gift is from God, and we must take our financial wealth with a humbled, gracious attitude. At the end of the day, we are still God's children and ambassadors.

God honors dreams that honor Him.

What is God calling you to do?

If you are unsure of the answer to that question, it's time to get into the Word. It's time to spend more time with God. God's ultimate priority in your life is a relationship with Him. He is wanting to use your testimony and your gifts to manifest miracles in your life, but it's more important to have a heart in line with His first. There are promises in scripture that must be cultivated in your heart so you are able to walk boldly in your purpose. God is calling us to assignments that seem impossible. That's because without Him, they are.

Rest in the Rainbow isn't just a book; it's a divine assignment. It's my God-sized dream. It is a dream that requires godly intervention in order to answer my prayers. It's a dream outside my means and resources. It's the leap of faith I am taking before I can see the open door. It's the seed God planted in my heart that requires me to trust that if the Lord has called me to it, He'll see it through. I rest in knowing that it is easy for God to open doors, and when God opens doors, it's impossible for anyone to shut them. God-sized dreams may seem impossible for us, but it's easy for Him. Miracles are God's nature, and God will use this book to build His Kingdom and bring glory to His name. If this book helps just one person find God, or helps just one person pursue the bigger and bolder plans God has already ordained for her or his life, then it is absolutely worth it. That "one person" might lead thousands to the Cross.

I hope and pray that it does, and I live expectantly that it will.

This is why we never underestimate the power of the seeds we are planting. Never underestimate the power of your God-given dream.

This is the promise that carried me throughout the work of writing this book: "Whatever you ask in my name, I will do it so that the Father may be glorified in the Son. If you ask me anything in my name, I will do it" (John 14:13–14).

God gives us the promises—it's up to us to claim them and invest in our purpose. May God bless you and carry you as you rest your heart in His promises.

Let His rainbow always be your reminder that he has never broken one, and never will.

BIBLIOGRAPHY

Batterson, Mark, *Chase the Lion* (The Crown Publishing Group, 2019).

Evans, Marshawn, *Believe Bigger* (Howard Books, 2019).

King, Martin Luther Jr., *Strength to Love* (Harper & Row, 1963).

Lowry, Lindy, "11 Christians Killed Every Day for Their Decision to Follow Jesus." March 13, 2019. https://www.opendoorsusa.org/christian-persecution/stories/11-christians-killed-every-day-for-their-decision-to-follow-jesus/

IMAGE Crux Dissimulata: http://www.articlemostwanted.com/2016/02/symbols-crows-foot-crucifix-crux.html#:~:text=CRUX%20DISSIMULATA%20In%20third-century%20Rome,%20early%20Christians%20were,to%20disguise%20the%20Cross%20skillfully%20as%20something%20else

Made in the USA
Monee, IL
29 November 2022